MINI
HOUSES

Art director: Claudia Martínez
Editorial coordination: Simone Schleifer
Editor and texts: Mariana R. Eguaras Etchetto
Layout: Ignasi Gracia Blanco
Translations (English, German, French, Dutch): Equipo de Edición

Editorial project:
2009 © **LOFT Publications**
Via Laietana, 32, 4.º, Of. 92
08003 Barcelona, Spain
Tel.: +34 932 688 088
Fax: +34 932 687 073
loft@loftpublications.com
www.loftpublications.com

ISBN 978-84-92731-03-9   Printed in China

MINI HOUSES

F K G

INTRODUCTION 08
EINLEITUNG
INTRODUCTION
INLEIDING

PROJECTS 12
PROJEKTE
PROJETS
PROJECTEN

TRENDS 582
TENDENZEN
TENDANCES
TRENDS

The last few decades have seen a boom in the development of small houses in response to the reduced size of families, the density of cities, the demands of today's citizens and the rise in price per square meter of property. These small homes present the perfect solution for busy professionals, married couples without children and adults who want to live alone or with their partner. Far from the concept of the last century, where importance and power were reflected by the size of a home, small houses (also known as 'mini-houses') have staked their claim in current architectural development.

In response to the increase in this type of small property, numerous companies and brands have created and developed products specifically for these compact spaces, marking a trend based on economy of resources and minimalist ideas.

INTRODUCTION

In den letzten Jahrzehnten gab es einen regelrechten Boom um kleine Wohnungen – eine Wohnform die auf Kleinfamilien, die Einwohnerdichte der Städte, die Bedürfnisse der heutigen Stadtbewohner sowie die Preissteigerungen des Immobilienmarktes reagiert. Diese kleinen Wohnungen stellen die perfekte Alternative für Berufstätige, kinderlose Paare oder Alleinstehende dar. Weit entfernt von den Vorstellungen des vergangenen Jahrhunderts, in dem eine große Wohnung als Statussymbol galt, vermochten es kleine Wohnungen (aufgrund ihrer starken Präsenz im englischsprachigen Raum auch „Mini-Wohnungen" oder „Mini Houses" genannt), sich in der aktuellen Architekturszene ihren eigenen Raum zu schaffen.

Als Reaktion auf den Boom der „Mini Houses" entwickelten verschiedene Unternehmen spezielle Produkte für diese kompakte Wohnform und schufen somit eine neue Tendenz, die auf Ökonomie und Minimalismus gründet.

EINLEITUNG

Si pendant des siècles, on a mesuré la position sociale et le pouvoir à l'aune des dimensions d'une habitation, la flambée des prix de l'immobilier comme des terrains à bâtir et la densité croissante de la population urbaine ont bousculé cette conception vieillotte. L'espace disponible en centre-ville étant de plus en plus restreint, y faire construire sa maison est également devenu rarissime. Autant de raisons qui expliquent l'engouement actuel pour les petits logements – urbains comme campagnards –, qui ont désormais leur place dans le panorama architectural contemporain.

Pour satisfaire cette demande, de nombreux architectes ont conçu des projets spécifiques, alliant économie de moyens et style dépouillé, voire minimaliste.

Le lecteur trouvera dans ces pages de nombreux exemples de petites maisons individuelles, où la recherche du confort malgré un espace réduit a conduit à d'astucieuses solutions d'aménagement comme de rangement.

INTRODUCTION

De laatste decennia zijn kleinere huizen, als antwoord op de kleiner wordende gezinnen, de bevolkingsdichtheid van steden, de eisen van de huidige stedelingen en de stijgende grondprijzen, als paddenstoelen uit de grond geschoten. Deze kleine woningen zijn een uitstekend alternatief voor druk bezette werkende mensen, stellen zonder kinderen en volwassenen die alleen of samen willen wonen.

Hoewel ver verwijderd van het concept van een eeuw geleden, waarin het belang en de waarde van een huis werden uitgedrukt in de grootte ervan, hebben kleine huizen (ook wel 'minihuizen' of, op zijn Engels, 'mini-houses') hun plek veroverd in de moderne architectonische ontwikkelingen.

In reactie op de groei van het aantal kleine woningen hebben verschillende bedrijven en merken speciale producten ontwikkeld voor dit soort compacte ruimten, waarmee een tendens is ontstaan gebaseerd op een beperkt budget en de ideologie van het minimalisme.

INLEIDING

ITAMAR'S CAVE

Itamar

Tel Aviv, Israel

© Undine Pröhl

DOMESPACE

Patrick Marsilli/DOMESPACE International

Quimper, France

77 m² / 829 sq ft

© Benjamin Thoby

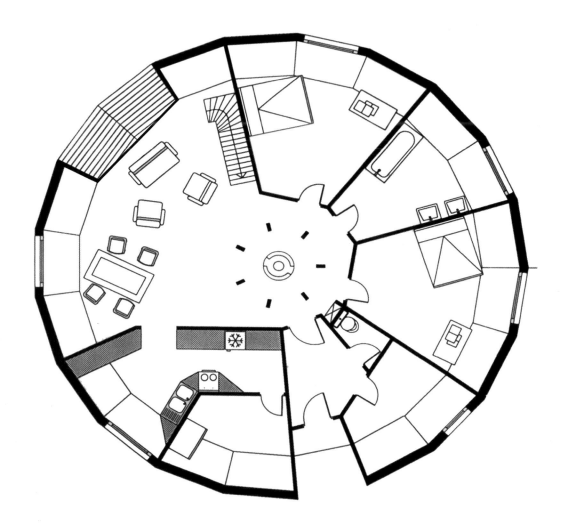

HOUSE IN TORRELLES

Rob Dubois

Torrelles de Llobregat, Spain

120 m² / 1,291 sq ft

© Jordi Miralles

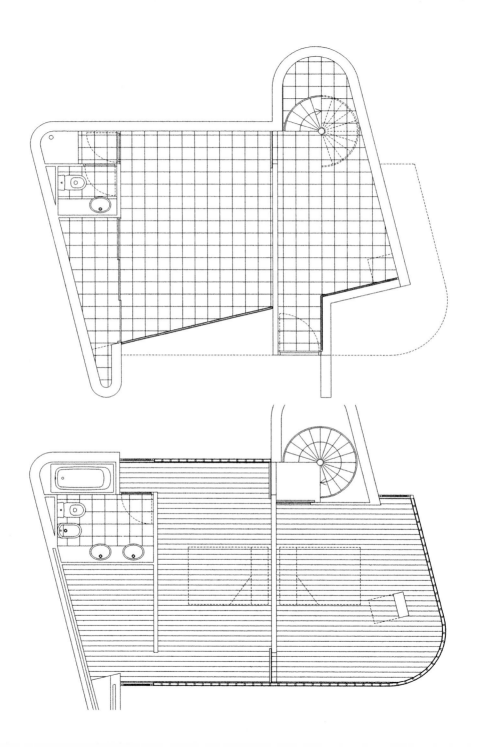

OFFICE HOUSE

Desai/Chia Studio

Bedford, United States

120 m² / 1,291 sq ft

© Joshua McHugh

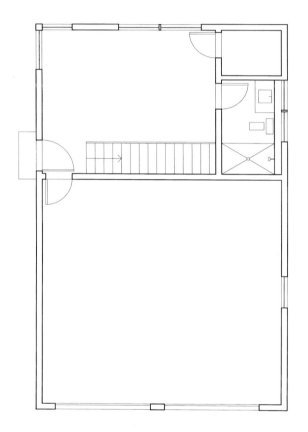

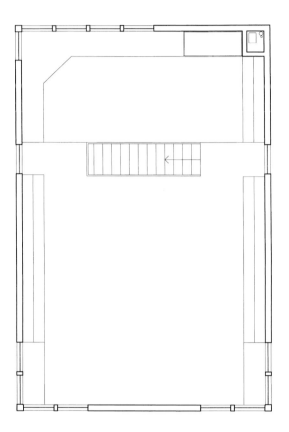

HOUSE ON MOUNT FUJI

Satoshi Okada

Yamanashi Prefecture, Japan

110 m² / 1,184 sq ft

© Hiroyuki Hirai

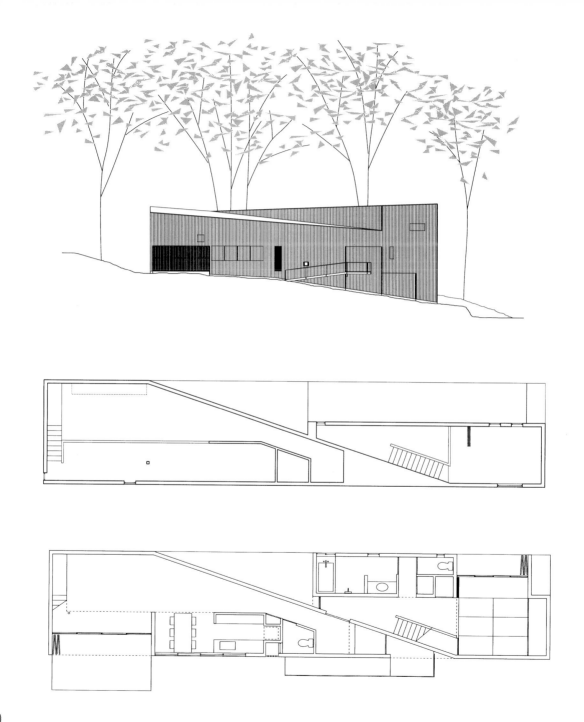

SUMMER RESIDENCE AND GALLERY

Henning Larsens Tegnestue

Vejby, Denmark

100 m² / 1,076 sq ft

© Jens Lindhe

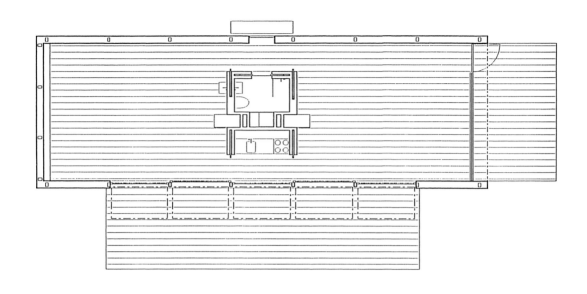

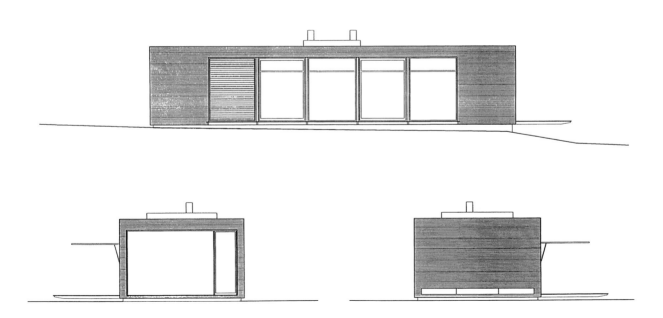

46

SOIVIO BRIDGE

Jukka Siren

Vammala, Finland

95 m^2 / 1,022 sq ft

© Lars Hallés, Arno de la Capelle

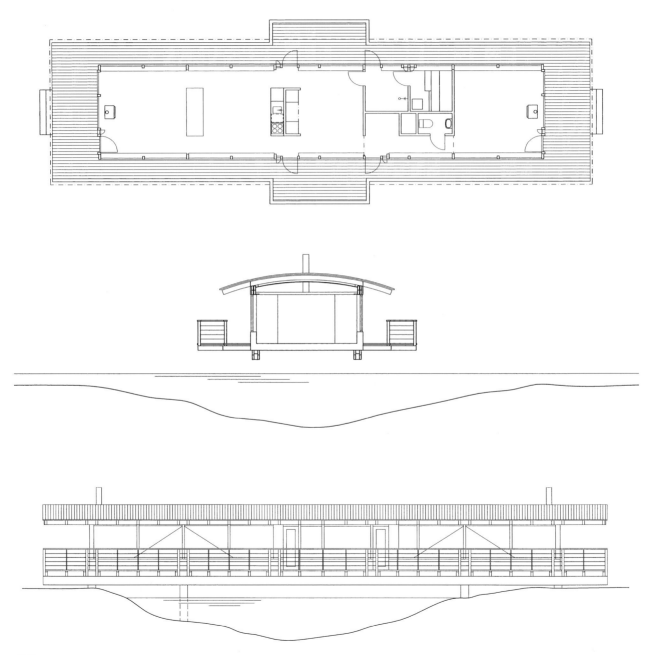

ITHACA HOUSE

Simon Ungers

Ithaca, United States

83 m² / 893 sq ft

© Eduard Hueber/Archphoto

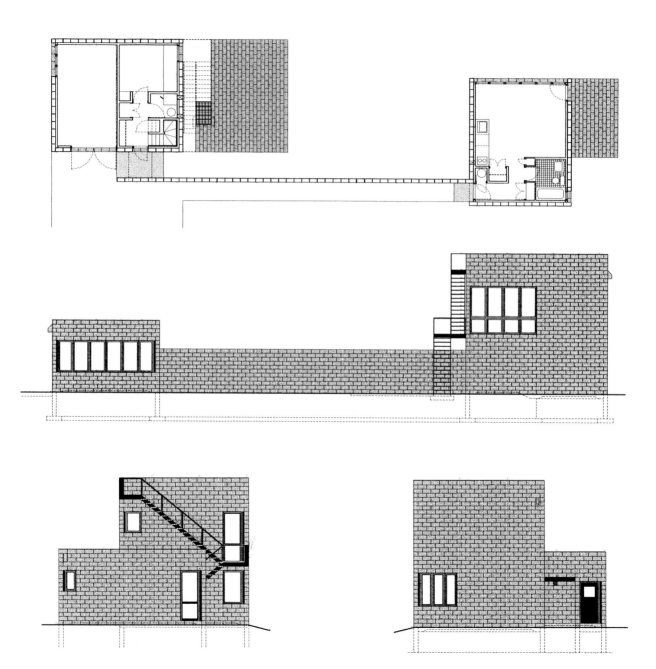

HOUSE ON THE ISLAND OMØ

Ole Holst

Island of Omø, Denmark

71 m² / 764 sq ft

© Ole Holst

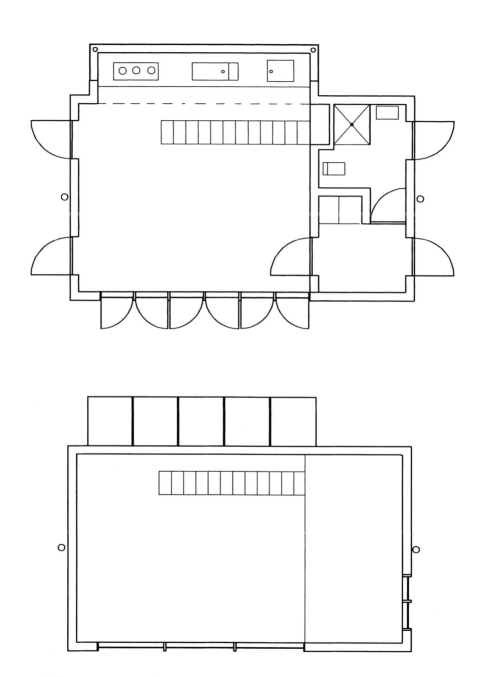

HOUSE BY THE SEA

Hanne Dalsgaard Jeppesen + Henrik Jeppesen Architects

Seeland, Denmark

77 m² / 828 sq ft

© Torben Eskerod

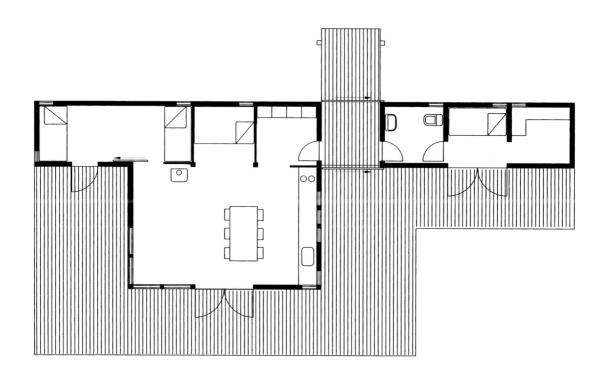

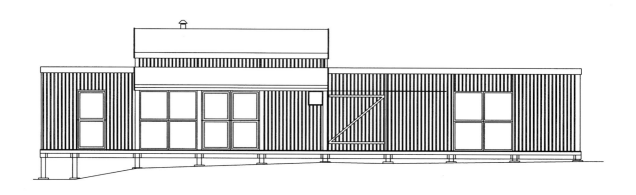

MOBILE HOUSE

Bauart Architects
Mobile
63 m^2 / 678 sq ft

© Andreas Greber, Haesle-Rüegsau

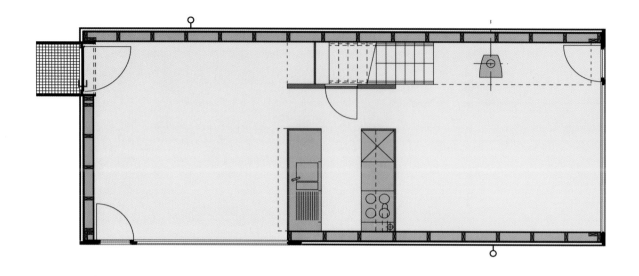

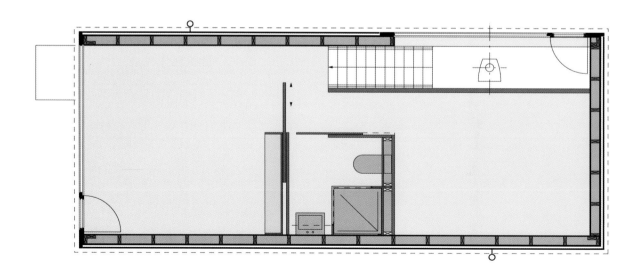

STUDIO 3773

Dry Designt
Los Angeles, United States
60 m² / 646 sq ft

© Undine Pröhl

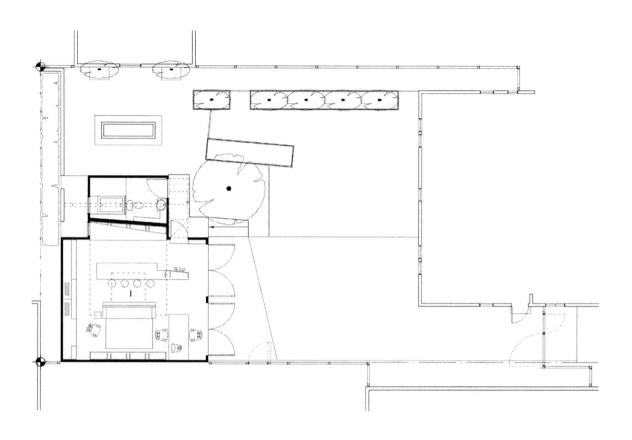

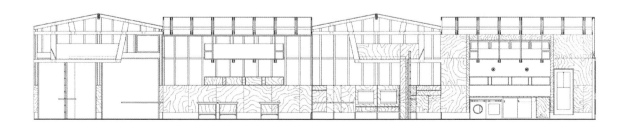

HOUSE IN ZACHARY

Stephen Atkinson

Louisiana, United States

51 m² / 549 sq ft

© Chipper Hatter

MINI HOME

Sustain Design Studio
Toronto, Canada
33 m² / 355 sq ft

© Sustain Design Studio

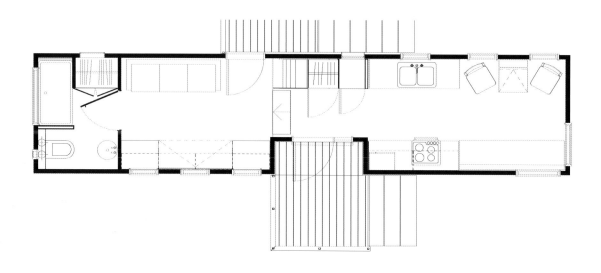

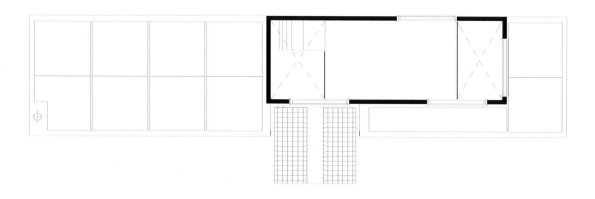

BLACK HOUSE

Andreas Henrikson

Halmstad, Sweden

33 m² / 355 sq ft

© Andreas Henrikson

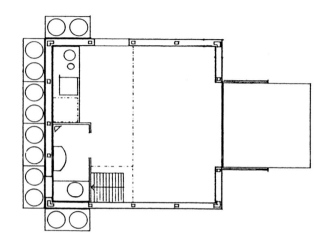

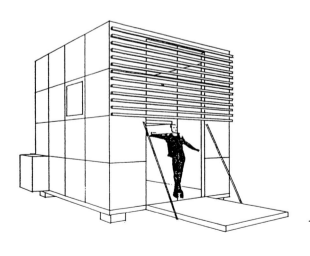

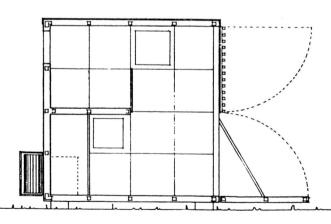

BALL HOUSE

Eduardo Longo

São Paulo, Brazil

100 m² / 1076 sq ft

© Fausto Ivan, Ana Carvalho

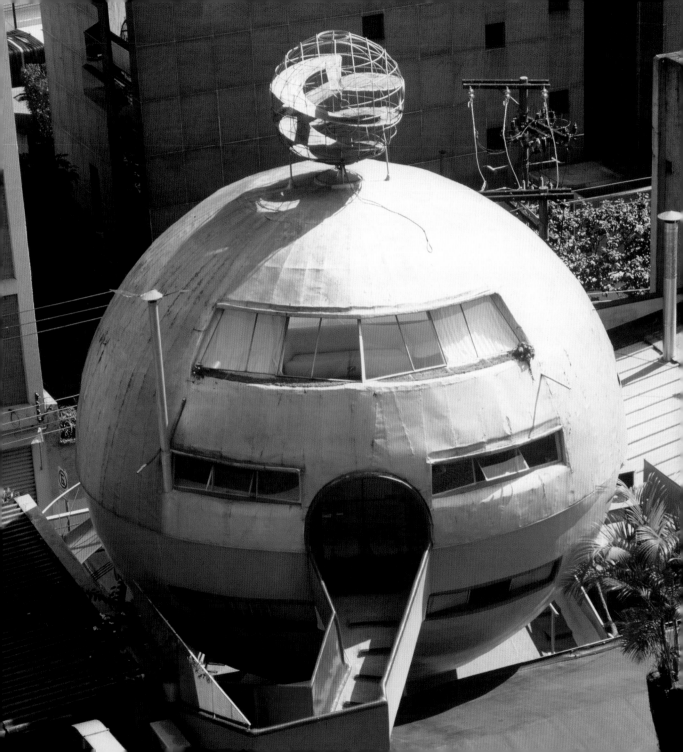

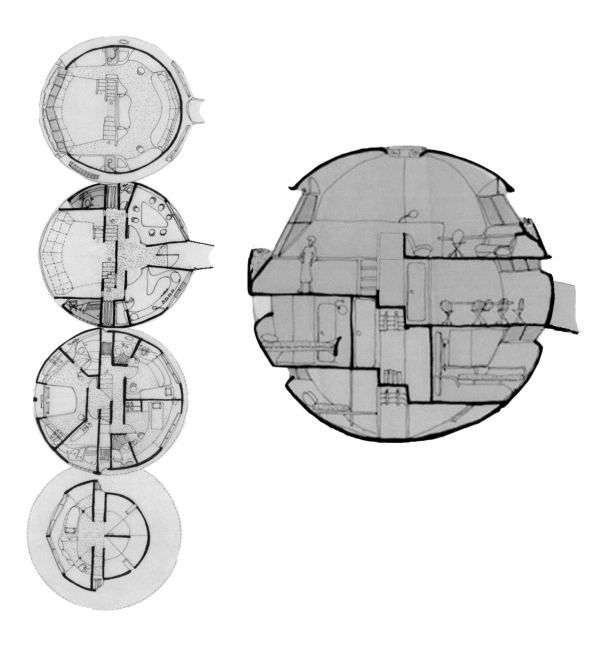

GUCKLHUPF

Architekurbüro Hans Peter Wörndl

Loibichl, Austria

48 m^2 / 517 sq ft

© Paul Ott

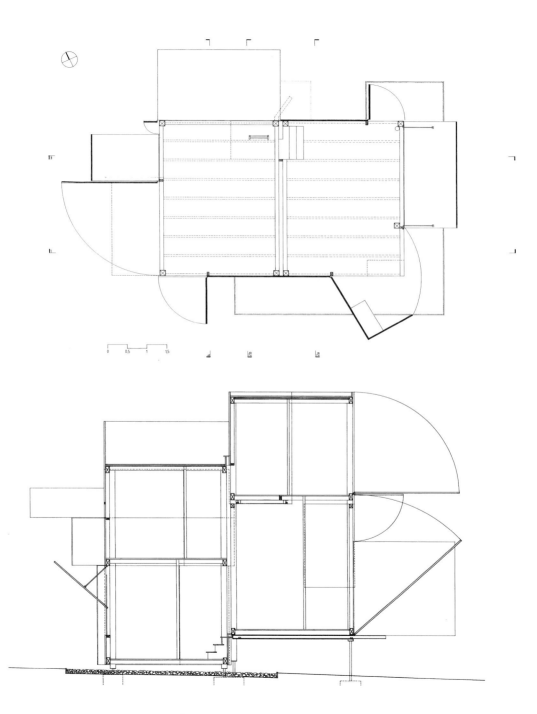

S•H•

Katsuhiro Miyamoto & Associates

Hyogo, Japan

103 ㎡ / 1,108 sq ft

© Kei Sugino

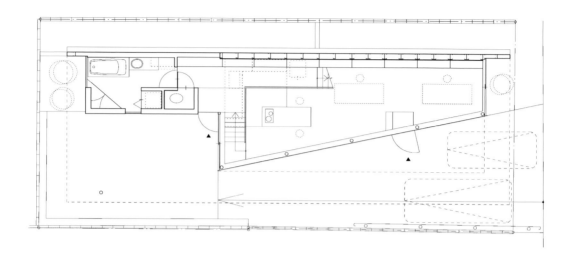

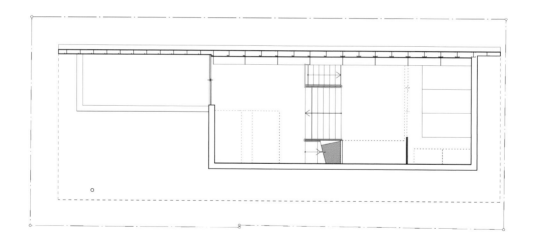

P•O•M EBISU

Rikuo Nishimori

Tokyo, Japan

117 m² / 1,259 sq ft

© Aki Furudate

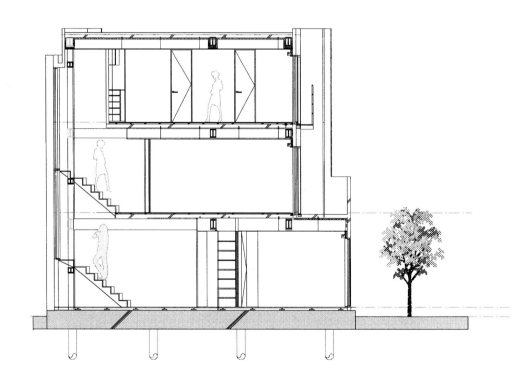

THREE HOUSES RATHMINES

Boyd Cody Architects, Paul Kelly/FKL Architects

Dublin, Ireland

100 m² / 1,076 sq ft

© Cillian Hayes

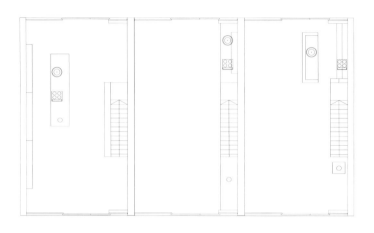

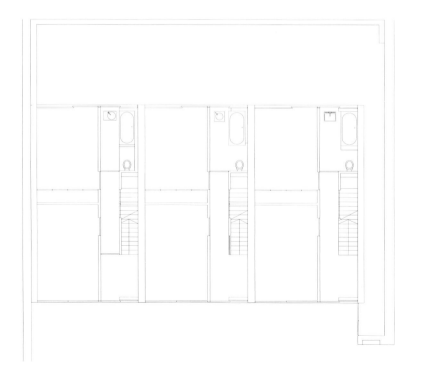

VILLA LINNANMÄKI

Risto Huttunen, Santeri Lipasti/Arkkitehtisuunnittelu Huttunen
& Lipasti

Somero, Finland

111 m² / 1,194 sq ft

© Marko Huttunen

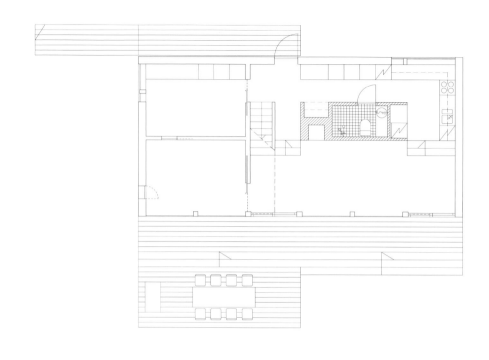

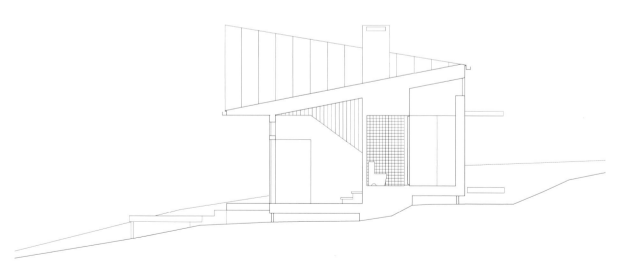

XXS

Dekleva Gregoric Arhitekti

Ljubljana, Slovenia

43 m² / 463 sq ft

© Matevz Pasternóster

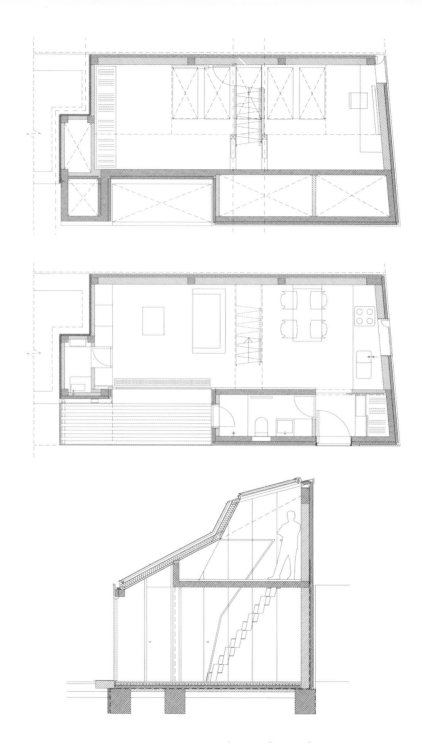

LEVIS HOUSE

UdA Studio & Davide Volpe

Vandorno, Italy

119 m² /1,280 sq ft

© Emilio Conti

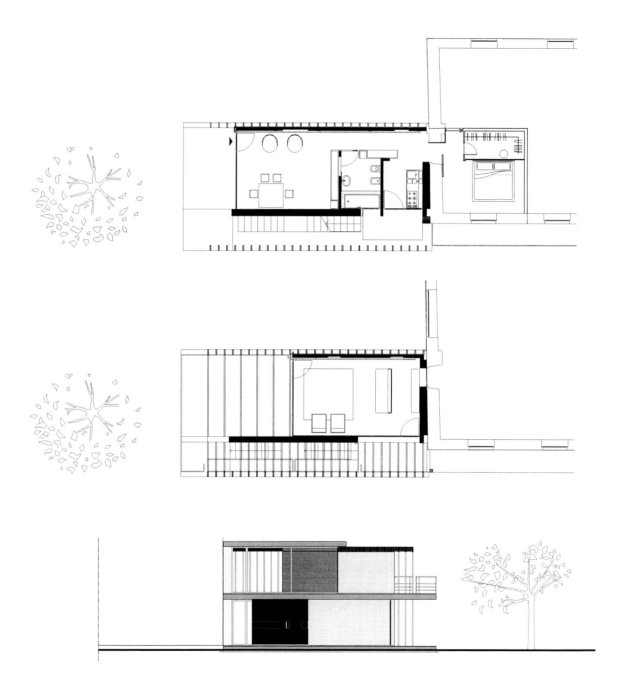

REFRACTION HOUSE

Kiyoshi Sey Takeyama

Nagoya, Japan

105 m^2 / 1,130 sq ft

© Yoshio Yiratori

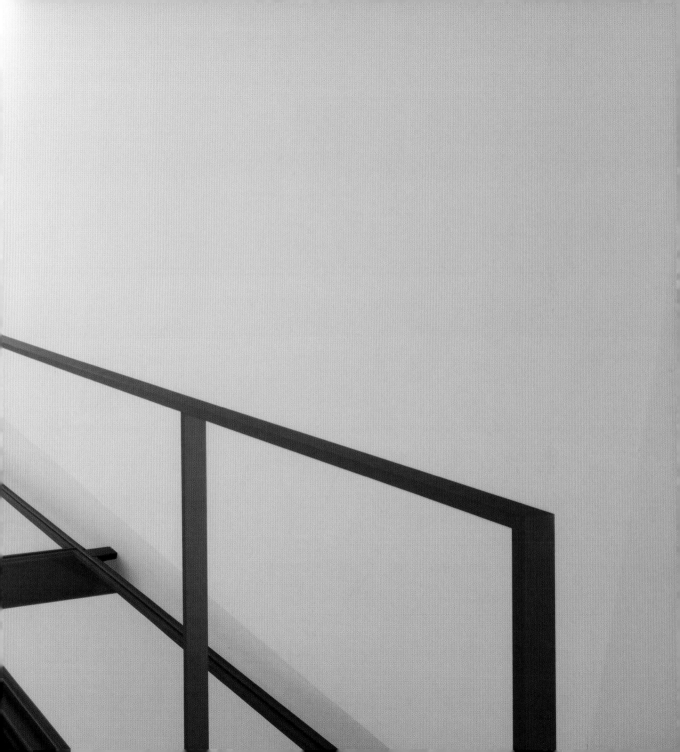

HOUSE IN CHELSEA

Rafael Berkowitz

New York, United States

© James Wilkins

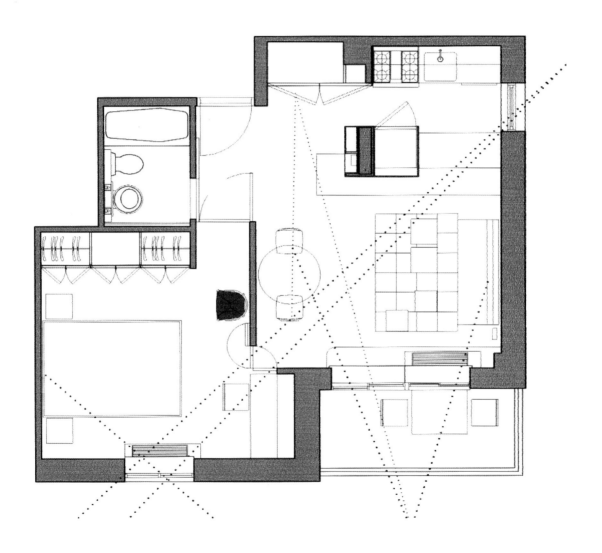

HOUSE IN MELBOURNE

Six Degrees Architects

Melbourne, Australia

80 m^2 / 861 sq ft

© Shania Shegedyn

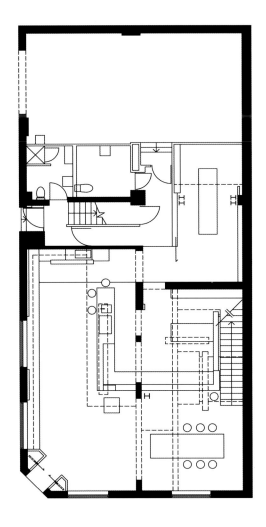

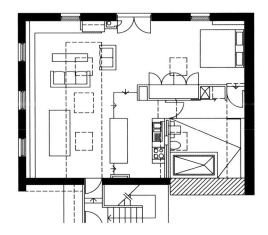

166

COCOON HOUSE

Michael Bellemo, Cat MacLeod

Wye River, Austria

68 m^2 / 732 sq ft

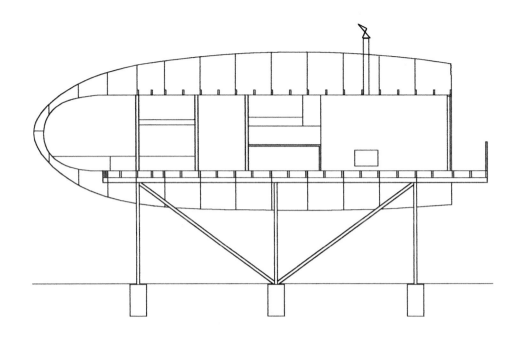

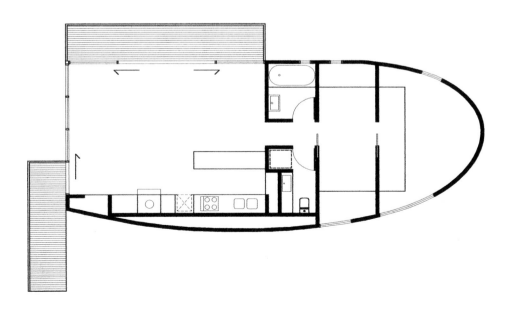

WEE RESIDENCE

Geoffrey Warner/Alchemy

Minnesota, United States

74 m² / 796 sq ft

© Douglas Fogelson

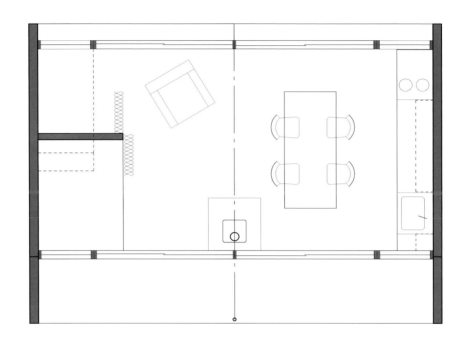

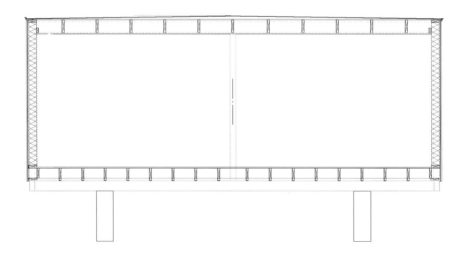

SEMPACHER HOMES

Camezind Evolution

Zurich, Switzerland

© Camezind Evolution

PIED-À-TERRE IN MIAMI BEACH

Pablo Uribe/Studio Uribe

Miami, United States

© Claudia Uribe

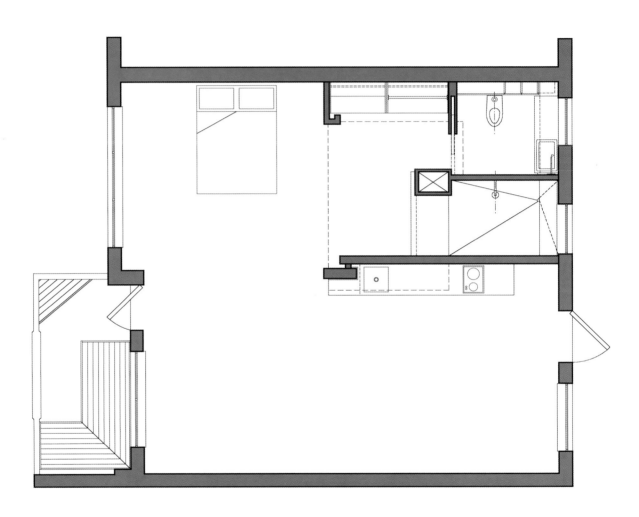

HOME IN LONDON

McDonell Associates

London, United Kingdom

© Carlos Domínguez

HANSE COLANI ROTOR HOUSE

Luigi Colani, Hanse Haus

Oberleichtersbach, Germany

36 m² / 387,5 sq ft

© Hanse Haus GmbH

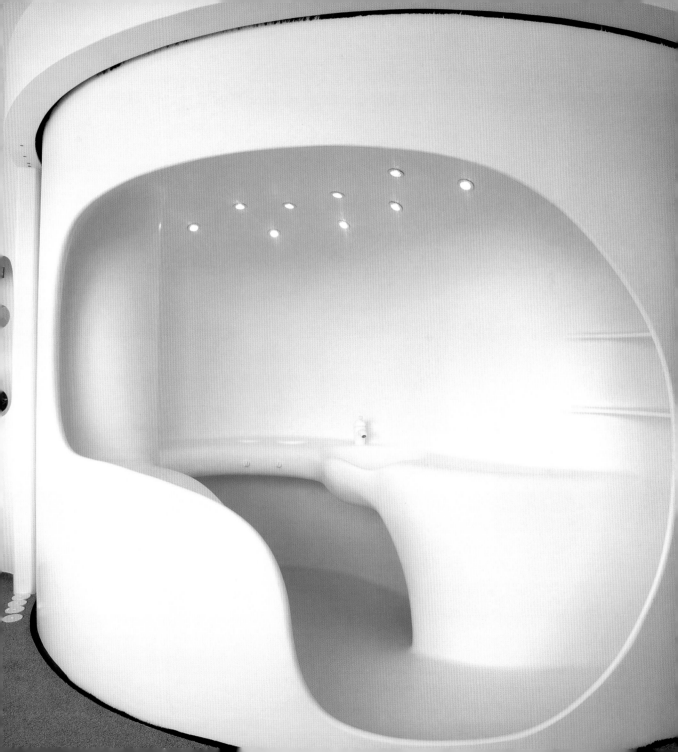

MICH MARONEY RESIDENCE

Michele Maroney

London, United Kingdom

© Carlos Domínguez

SLIT VILLA

C. Matsuba/tele-design

Tokyo, Japan

67 m² / 721 sq ft

© Ryota Atarashi

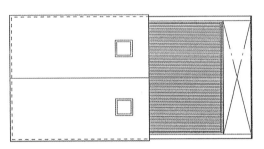

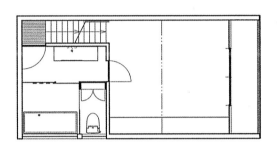

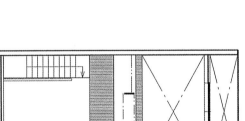

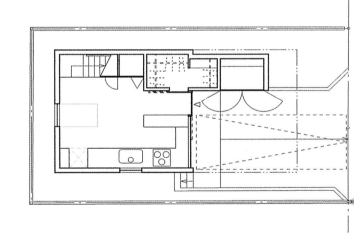

214

TAVOLA

Milligram Studio

Saitama, Japan

78 m^2 / 840 sq ft

© Takeshi Taira

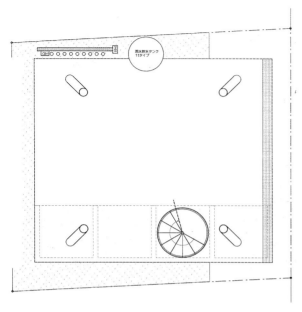

雨水貯水タンク
1tタイプ

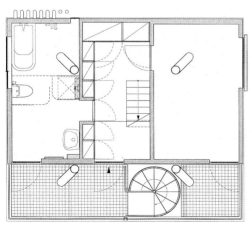

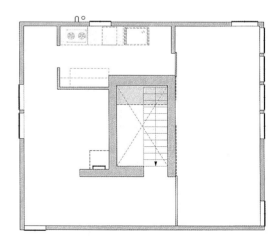

220

PIXEL HOUSE

Slade Architecture and Mass Studies
Heiri, South Korea
85 m² / 915 sq ft

© Kim Yong Kwan

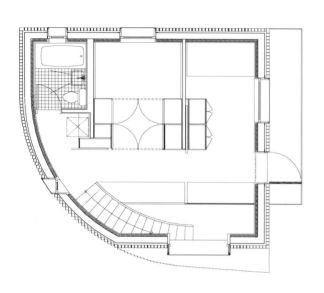

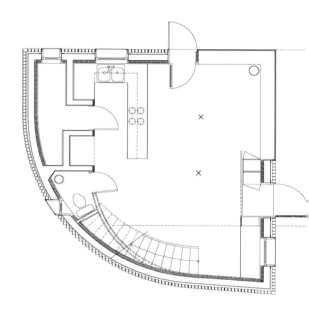

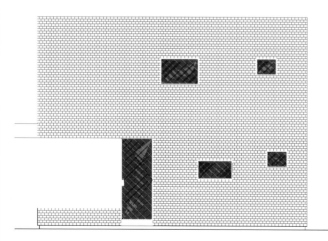

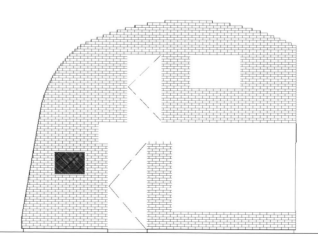

WHITE RIBBING

Milligram Studio

Tokyo, Japan

89 m² / 958 sq ft

© Takeshi Taira

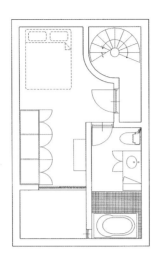

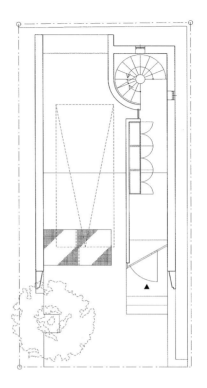

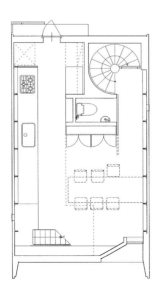

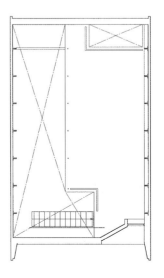

ROOFTECTURE M

Shuhei Endo

Maruoka-cho, Japan

95 m^2 / 1,023 sq ft

© Yoshiharu Matsumara

住いの提案

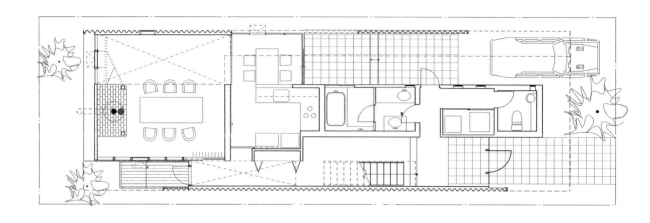

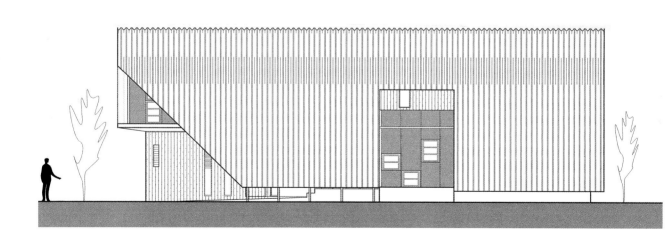

CLARABOYA HOUSE

Flemming Skude

Lolland, Denmark

78 m^2 / 840 sq ft

© Flemming Skude

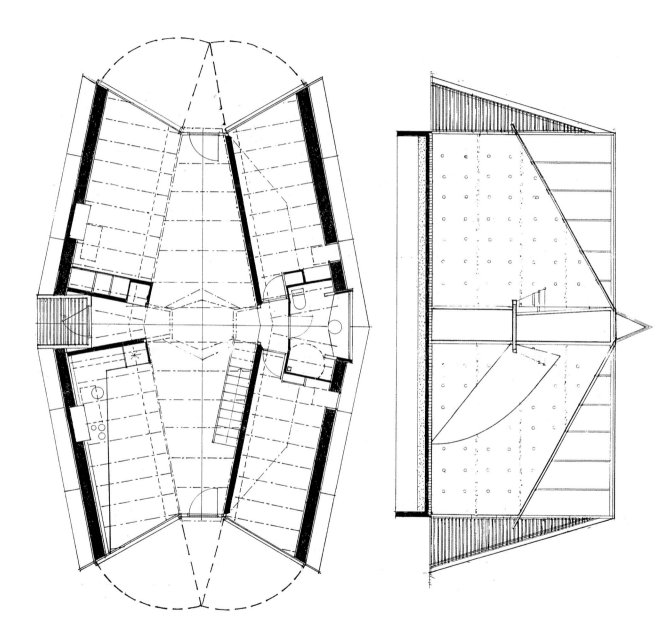

244

PREFABRICATED REFUGES

Geoffrey Warner/Alchemy

Two Harbours, United States

70 m² / 753 sq ft

© Geoffrey Warner/Alchemy

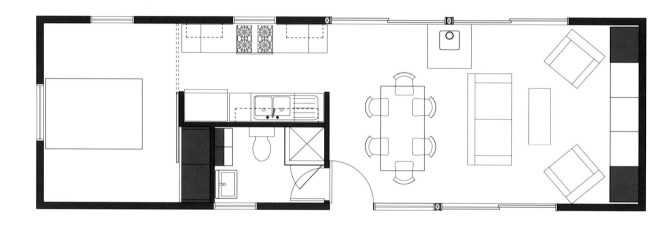

250

M-HOUSE

Michael Jantzen

Gorman, United States

93 m² / 1,001 sq ft

© Michael Jantzen

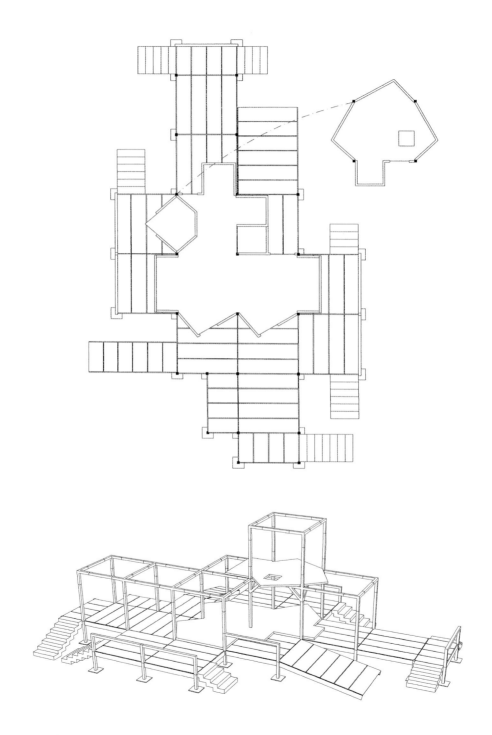

ENGELS-HOUBEN PASIVE HOUSE

Rongen Architekten

Rurich, Germany

© Rongen Architekten

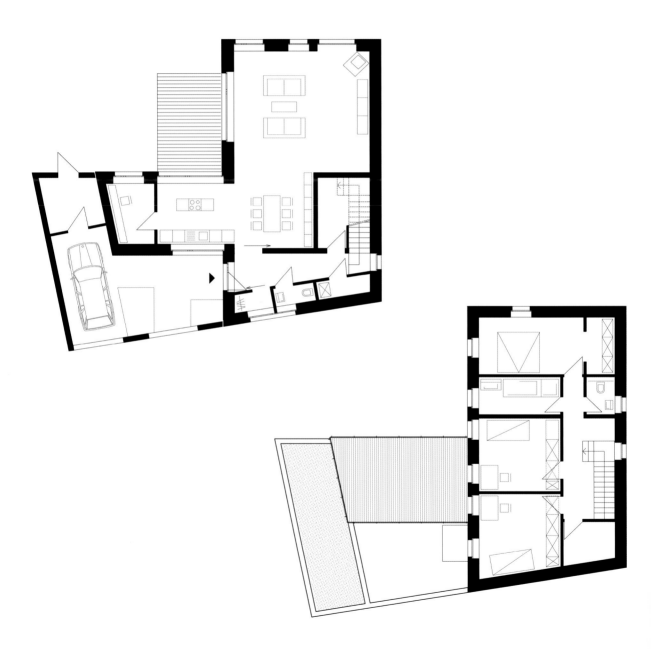

LIVINGSCAPE

Graeme North Architects

Warkworth, New Zealand

© Graeme North Architects

MODERN CABANA

Casper Mork-Ulnes/Modern Cabana Co.

Throughout the Unites States

9,3 m² / 100 sq ft

© Bruce Damonte

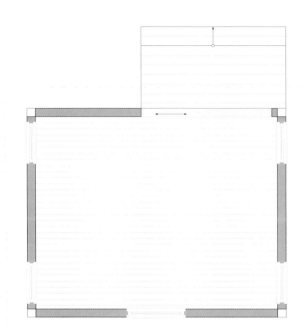

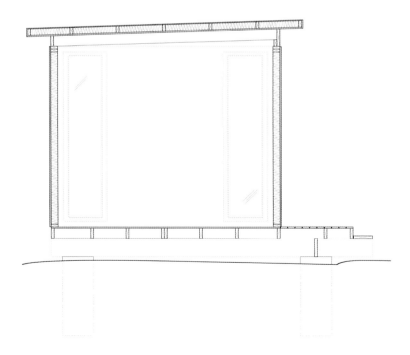

VERTICAL HOUSE

Lorcan O'Herlihy

Venice, United States

© Undine Pröhl

WEEBEE

Jay Shafer/Tumbleweed Tiny Houses Company
Mobile
10,20 m² / 110 sq ft

© Jay Shafer

SOCCER BALL-SHAPED HOUSE

Kimidori Housing

Gifu, Japan

50 m² / 540 sq ft

© Kimidori Housing

KITHAUS K3

Tom Sandonato & Martin Wehmann/Design Within Reach

Anywhere

11 m² / 117 sq ft

© Kithaus/Design Within Reach

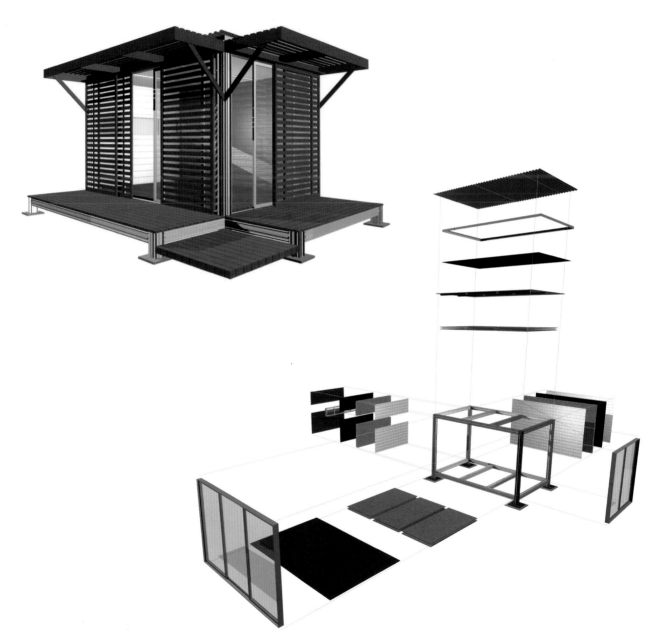

SEATRAIN HOUSE IN LOS ANGELES

Jennifer Siegal

Los Angeles, United States

© Undine Pröhl

RESIDENCE IN SYDNEY

Marsh Cashman Architects

Los Angeles, United States

© Willem Rethmeier

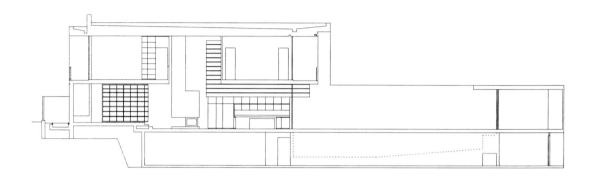

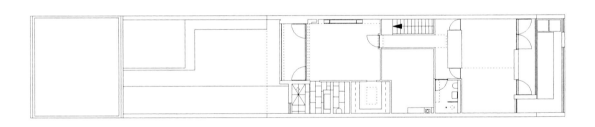

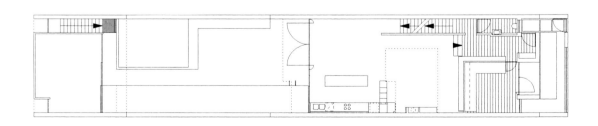

LAYER HOME

Hiroaki Ohtani

Sydney, Australia

33 m² / 355 sq ft

© Kouji Okamoto

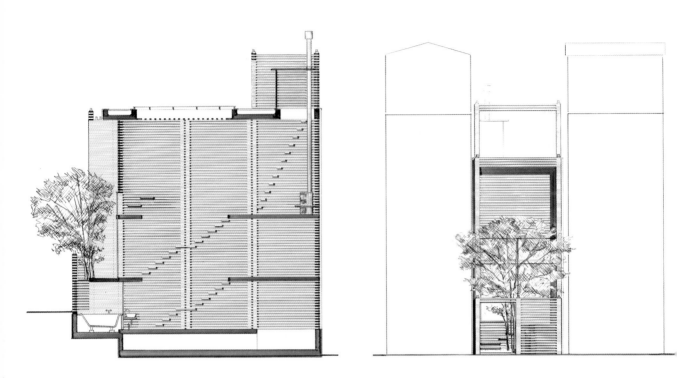

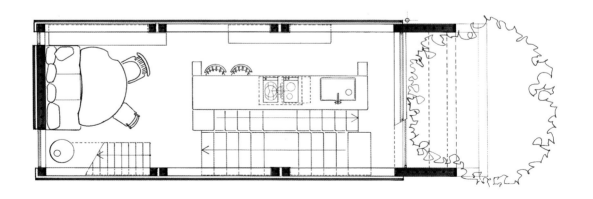

316

RESIDENCE IN MELBOURNE

John Wardle Architects

Melbourne, Australia

© Trevor Mein

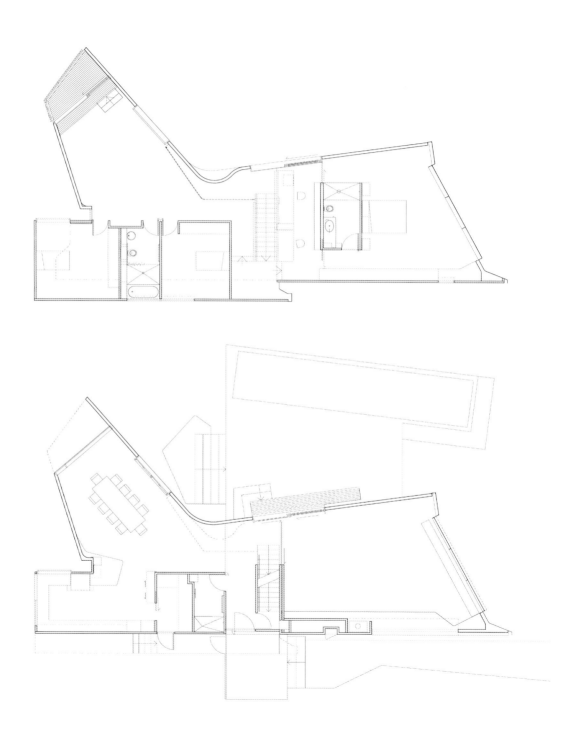

MINI-HOUSE

Atelier Bow Bow

Linz, Austria

27,40 m² / 290 sq ft

© Shigeru Hiraga

TELEGRAPH HILL RESIDENCE

House & House Architects

San Francisco, United States

© Willem Rethmeier

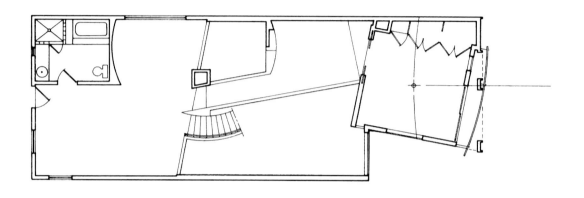

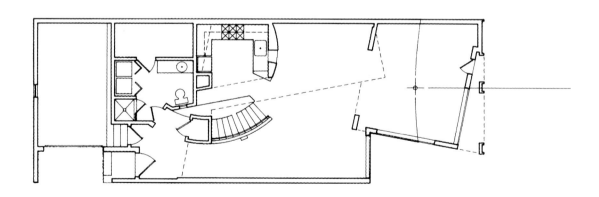

FOLD HOUSE

Mutsue Hayakusa/Cell Space Architects

Nagareyama, Japan

94 m² / 1,012 sq ft

© Satoshi Asakawa

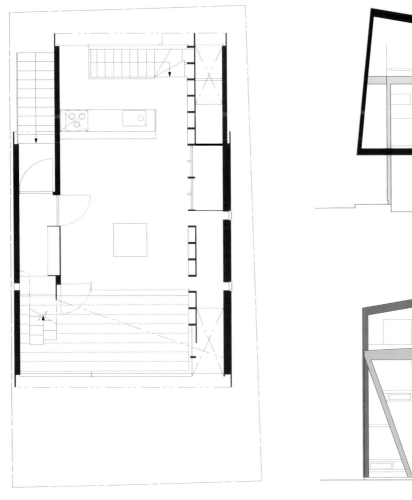

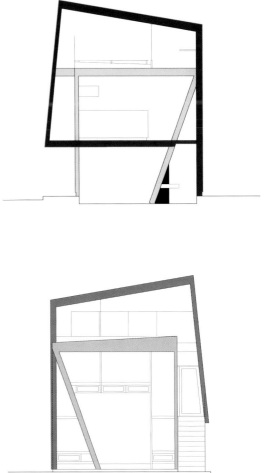

HAUS P

Thaler Architekten

Vienna, Austria

100 m² / 1,076 sq ft

© Hr. Sina Baniahmad

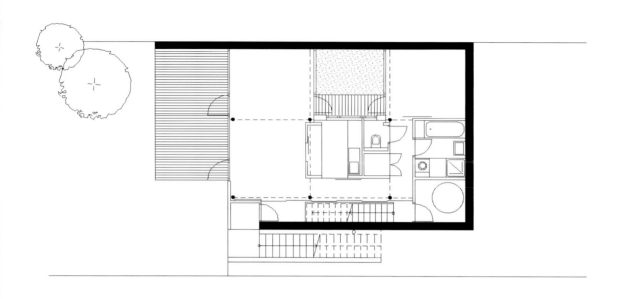

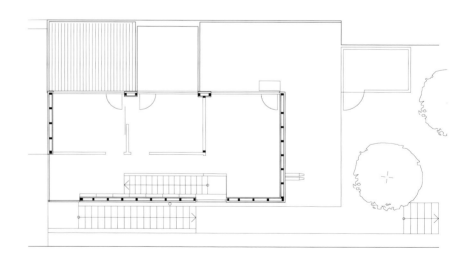

018

Hiroyuki Arima + Urban Fourth

Kanagawa, Japan

102 ㎡ / 1,098 sq ft

© Kouji Okamoto

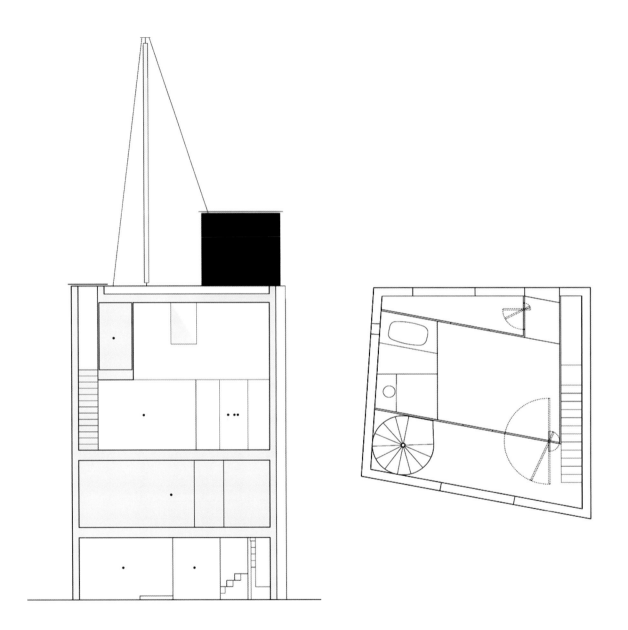

HOUSE IN SETAGAYA

NAYA Architects: Manabu + Arata
Setagaya, Japan
106 ㎡ / 1,141 sq ft

© Makoto Yoshida

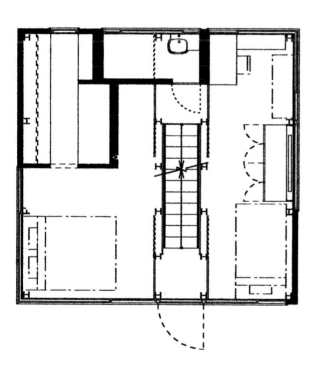 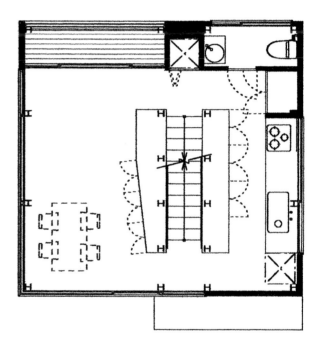

HOUSE IN MOTOAZABU

Mutsue Hayakusa/Cell Space Architects

Tokyo, Japan

112 m² / 1,206 sq ft

© Satoshi Asakawa

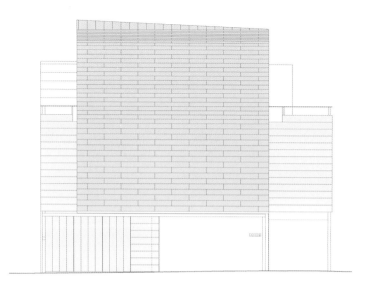

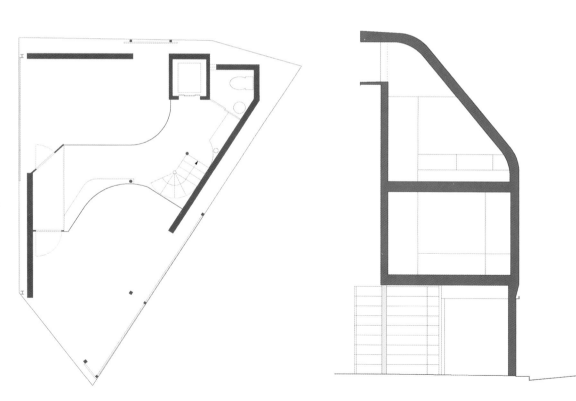

KASSAI HOUSE

Kiyoshi Sey Takeyama + Amorphe

Osaka, Japan

116 m² / 1,249 sq ft

© Koichi Torimura

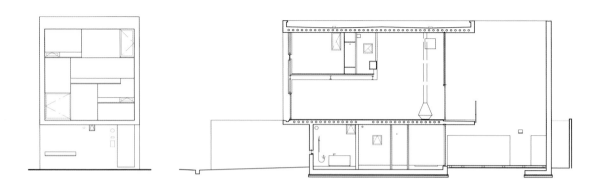

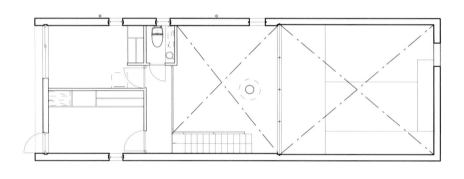

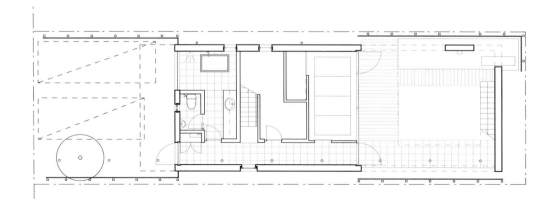

CLAUDIA BRUCKNER RESIDENCE

Hans-Peter Lang

Rankweil, Austria

70 m^2 / 753 sq ft

© Albrecht Schnabel

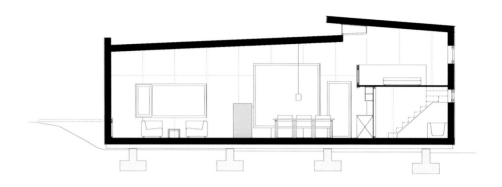

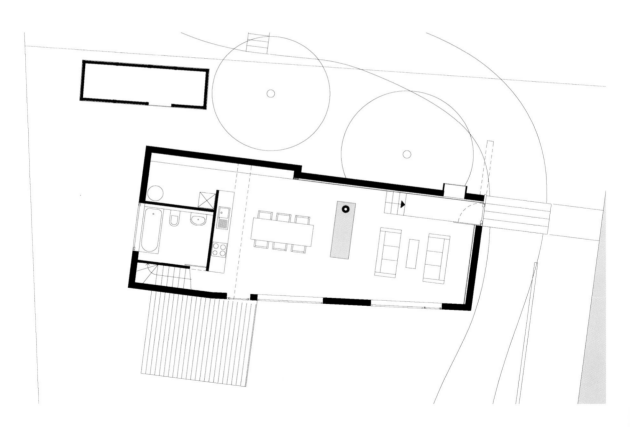

MINIMAL HOUSE

Ivan Kroupa

Mukarov, Czech Republic

72 m² / 775 sq ft

© Matteo Piazza

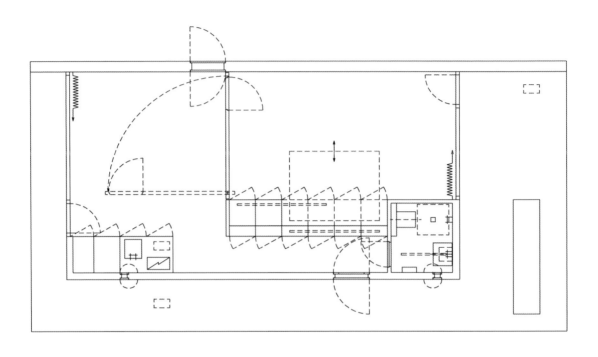

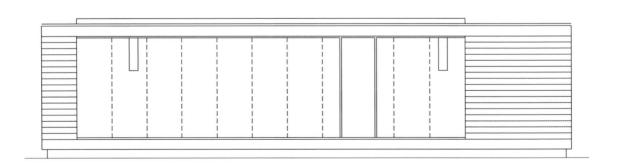

A HOUSE IN THE GARDEN

Archteam

Kromeriz, Czech Republic

75 m² / 807 sq ft

© Ester Havlova

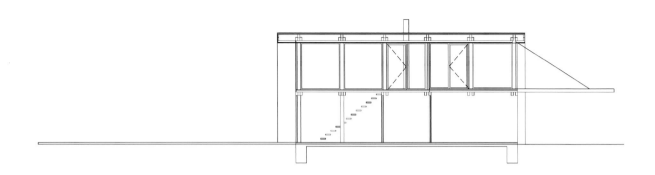

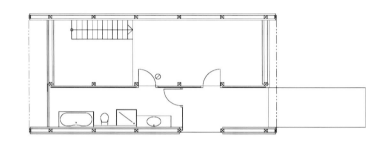

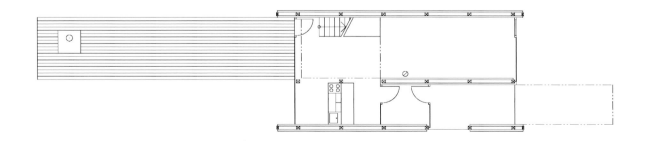

SINGLE-FAMILY HOME

Esteve Terrades

Gaüses de Dalt, Spain

98 m² / 1,055 sq ft

© Jordi Canosa

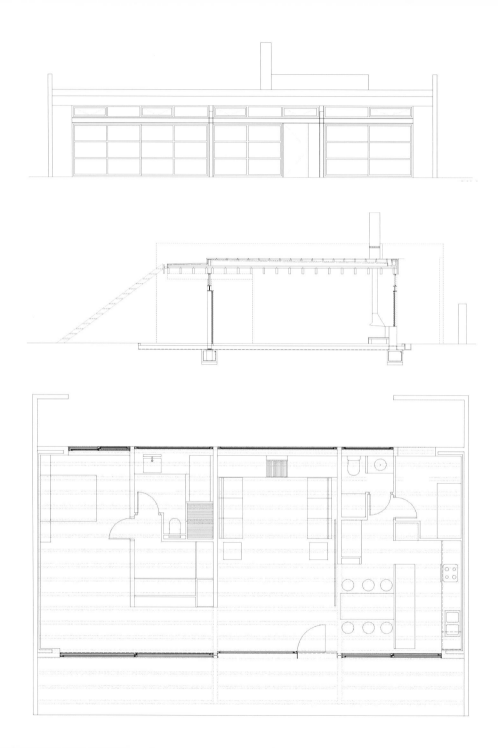

4X4 HOUSE

Tadao Ando Architect & Associates

Hyogo, Japan

118 m² / 1,270 sq ft

© Mitsuo Matsuoka

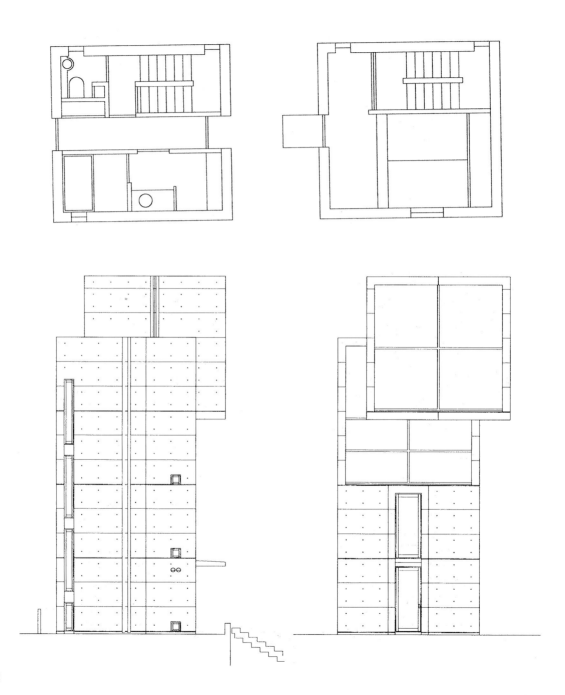

SOLAR BOX

Driendl Architects

Vienna, Austria

80 m² / 861 sq ft

© Lew Rodin

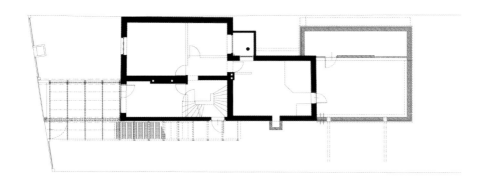

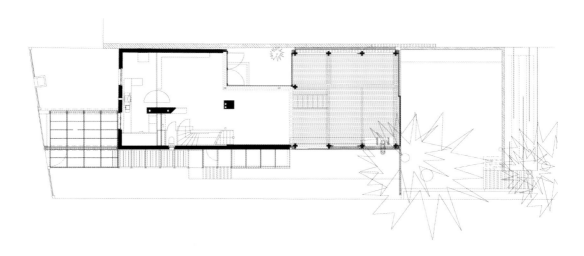

ZENZMAIER HOUSE

Maria Flöckner and Hernann Schnöll

Kuchl, Austria

102 m² / 1,098 sq ft

© Stefan Zenzmaier

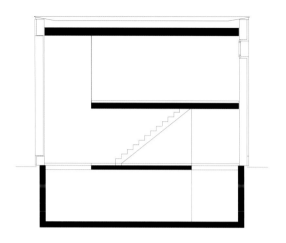

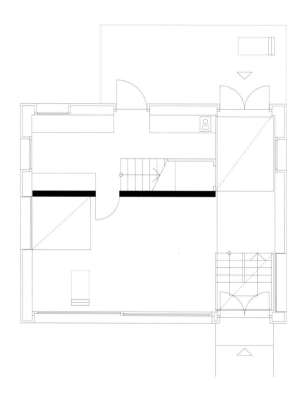

BOATHOUSE

Drew Heath

Sydney, Australia

35,50 m² / 377 sq ft

© Brett Boardman

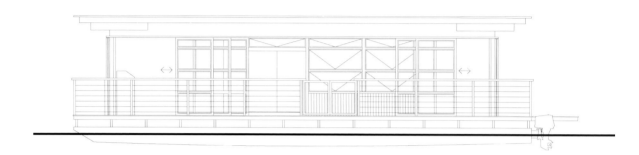

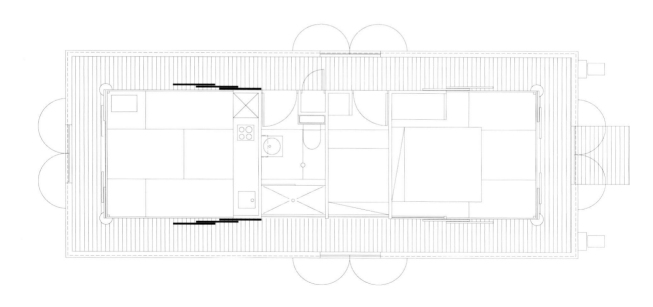

418

BOX HOUSE

Nicholas Murcutt/Neeson Murcutt Architects

Tathara, Australia

50 m² / 538 sq ft

© Brett Boardman

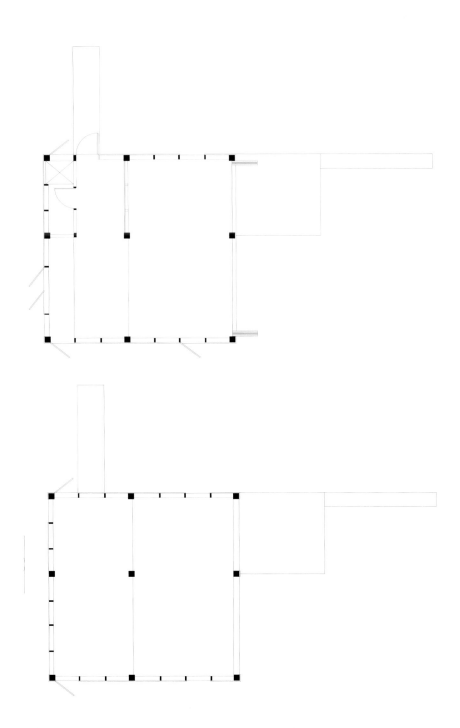

424

HOUSE IN CARRASCAL

Mariano Martín
Carrascal de la Cuesta, Spain
110 m² / 1,184 sq ft

© Pedro López Cañas

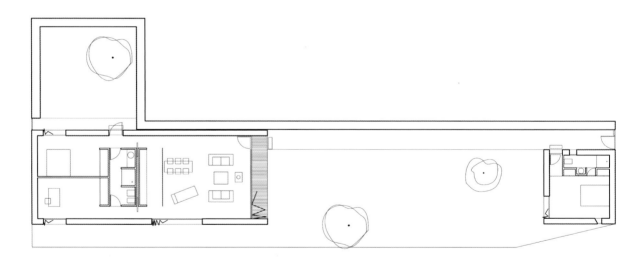

C-2 HOUSE

Curiosity

Yamanashi, Japan

46 ㎡ / 495 sq ft

© Gwenael Nicolas/Curiosity

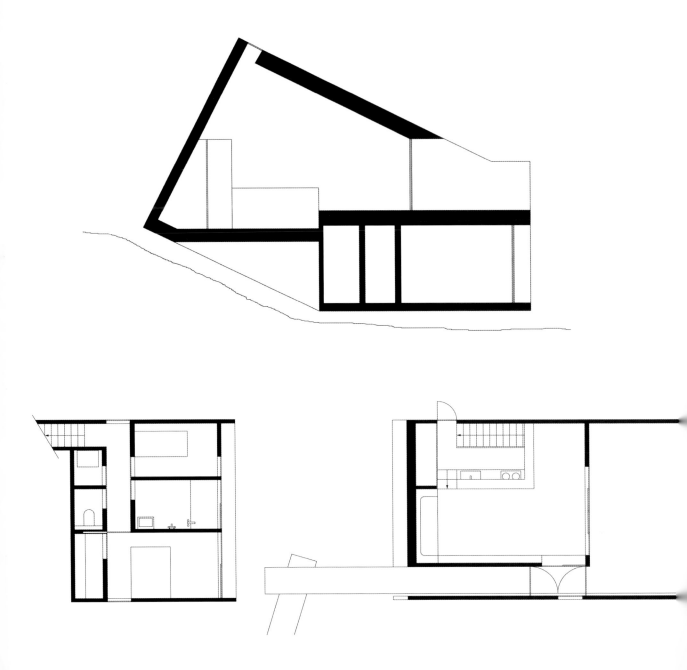

O-HOUSE

CUBO Architects

Matsumoto, Japan

62 m² / 667 sq ft

© Yasuno Sakata

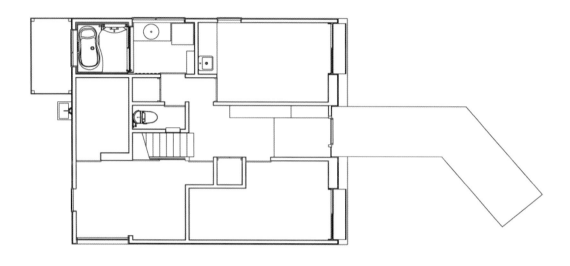

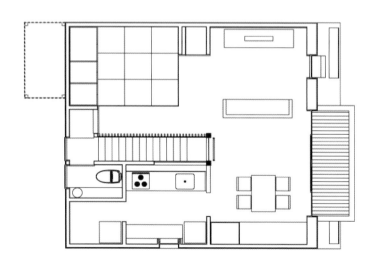

LOFTCUBE

Studio Aisslinger

Berlin, Germany

39 m^2 / 420 sq ft

© Steffen Jänicke Fotografie

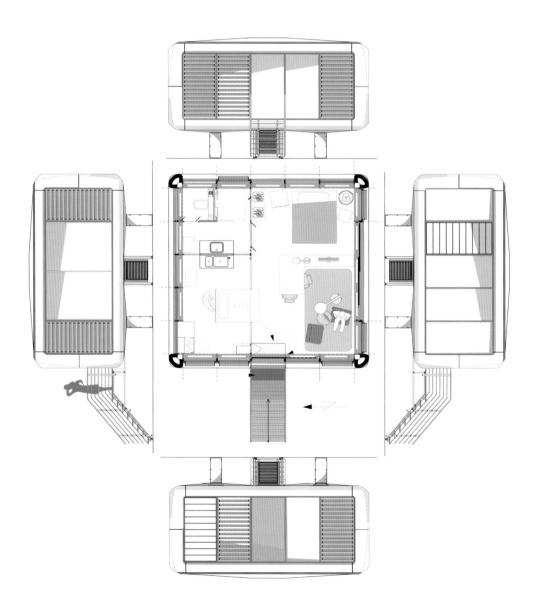

PREFAB HOUSE IN DENMARK

ONV Architects
Vanlose, Denmark
86 m² / 925 sq ft

© Station 1

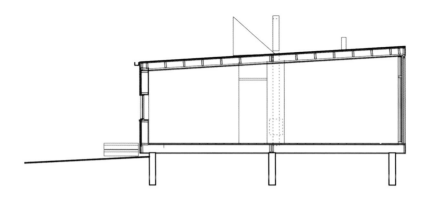

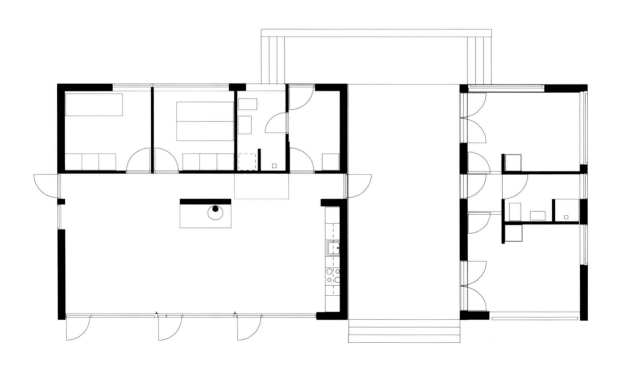

MK LOTUS

Michelle Kaufmann Designs

San Francisco, United States

65 m² / 700 sq ft

© Michelle Kaufmann Designs

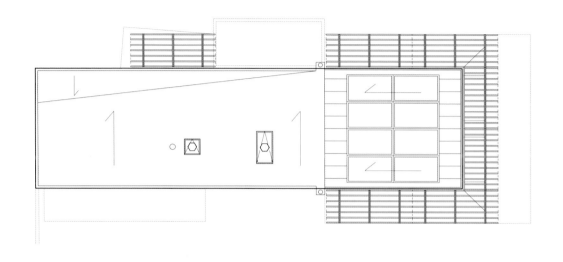

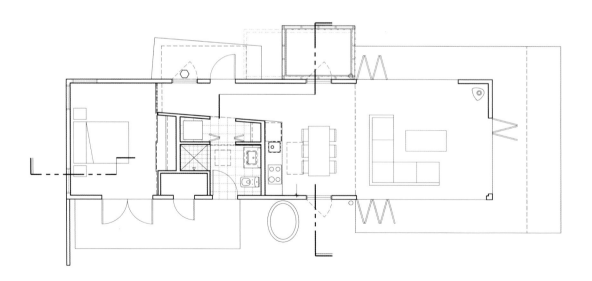

460

MICRO COMPACT HOME

Horden Cherry Lee Architects, Haack Höpfner Architekten

Munich, Germany

7 m² / 75 sq ft

© Sascha Kletzsch

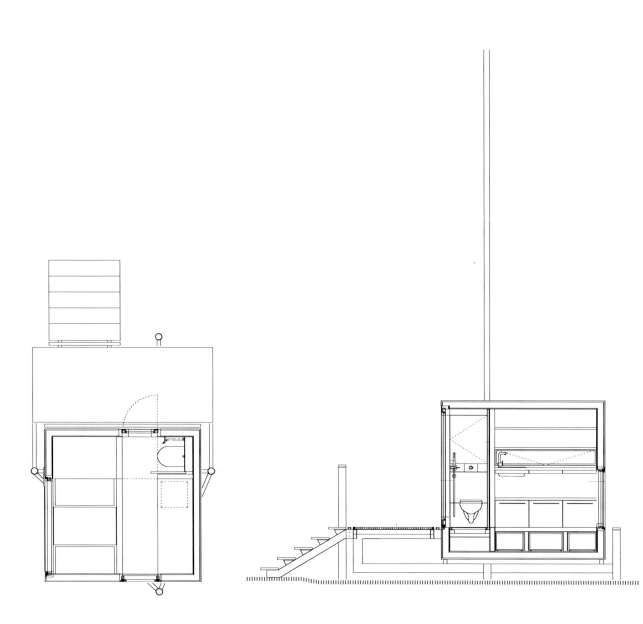

HENDELKENS PASIVE HOUSE

Rongen Architekten

Hückelhoven, Germany

138 m² / 1,485 sq ft

© Rongen Architekten

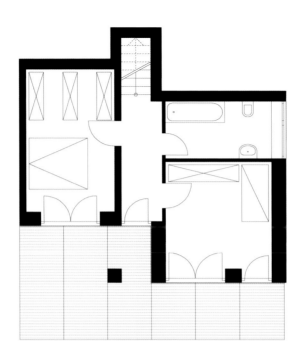

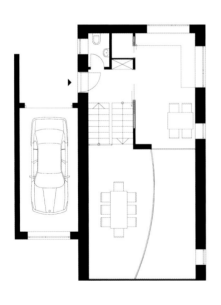

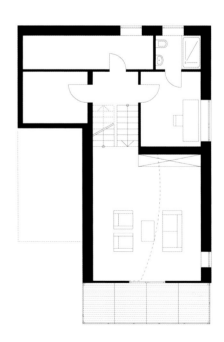

472

LAVAFLOW2

Craig Steely

Hawaii, United States

130 m² / 1,400 sq ft

© JD Peterson

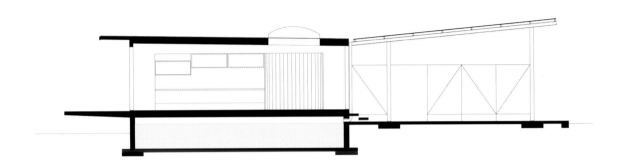

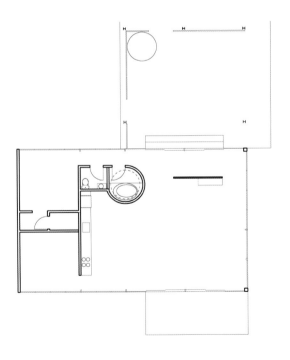

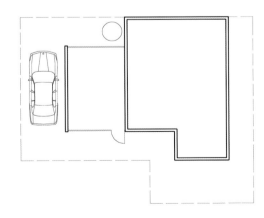

WINE CREEK ROAD RESIDENCE

Siegel & Stein Architects

Healdsburg, United States

© JD Peterson

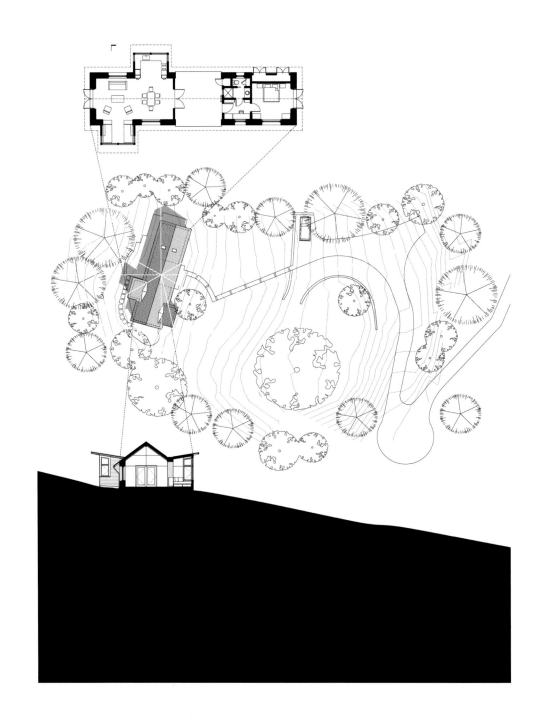

RUBISSOW FARM

Okamoto Saijo Architecture

Napa Valley, United States

111 m² / 1,200 sq ft

© Janet Delaney

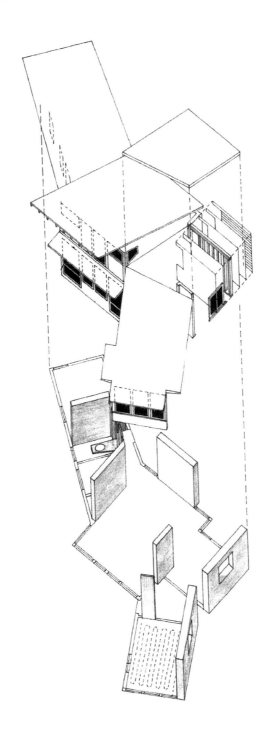

490

PARKSTRAßE HOUSE

Rongen Architekten
Wassenberg, Germany

© Rongen Architekten

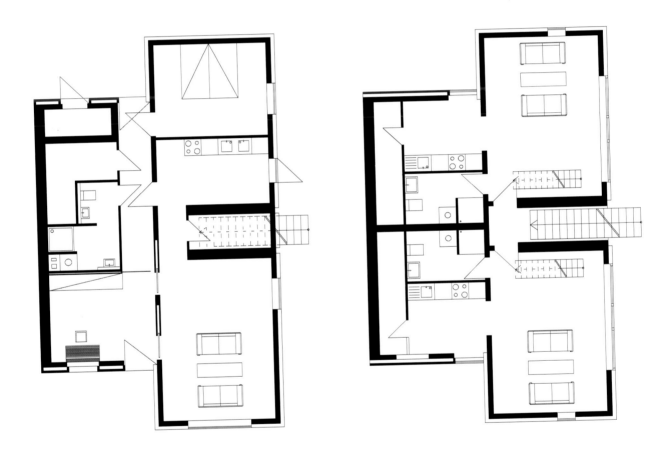

SOLARHAUS II

GLASSX AG, Dietrich Schwarz

Ebnat-Kappel, Switzerland

© Frédérik Comptesse

FUJY HOUSE

Fujy - Arquitectura por naturaleza

El Escorial, Spain

© Miguel de Guzmán

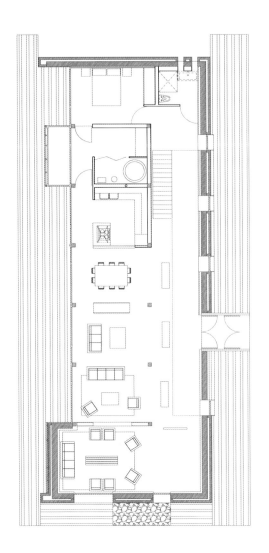

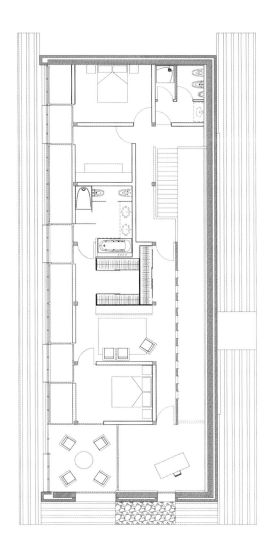

508

CABIN IN CHICKEN POINT

Olson Sundberg Kundig Allen Architects

Idaho, United States

54 m^2 / 581 sq ft

© Undine Pröhl

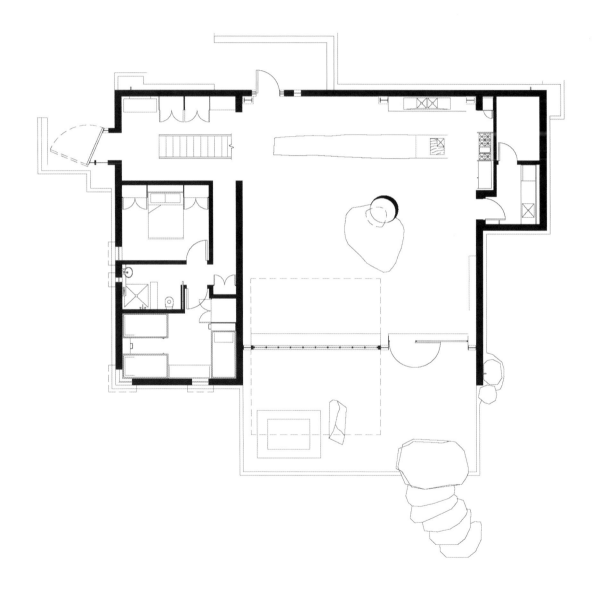

514

ATELIER IN THE MOUNTAIN

Toshihiro Suzuki

Japan

© Toshihiro Suzuki

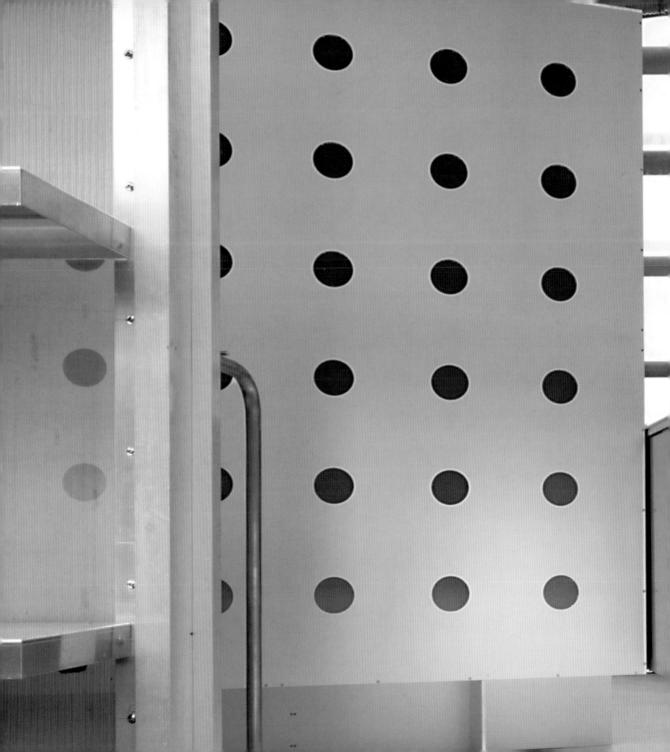

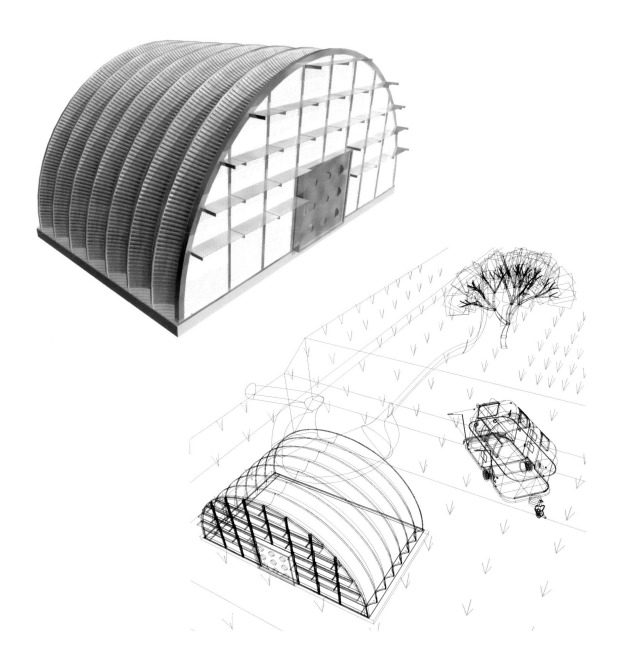

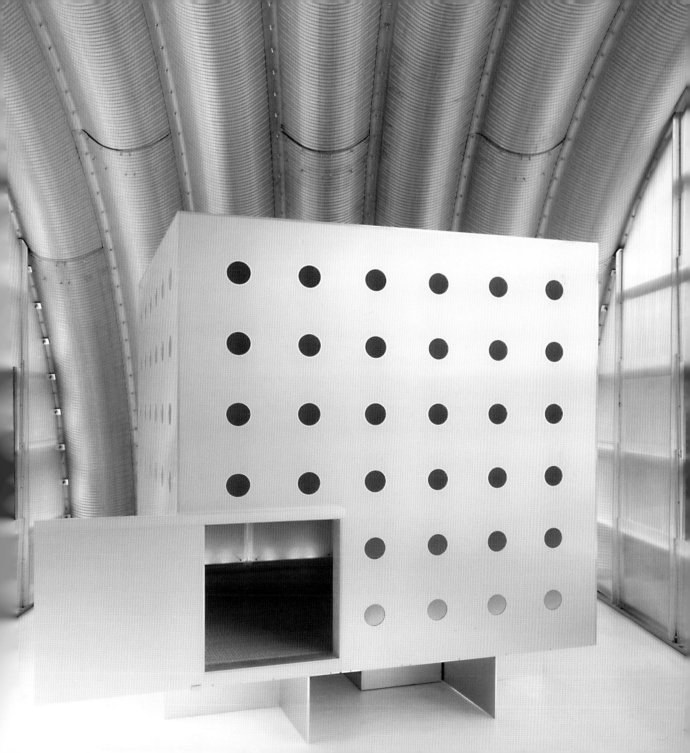

HO & HO

Happy Linving

Milan, Italy

KAPS HOUSE

Caramel Architekten

Saalfelden am Steineren Meer, Austria

84 m^2 / 904 sq ft

© Caramel Architekten

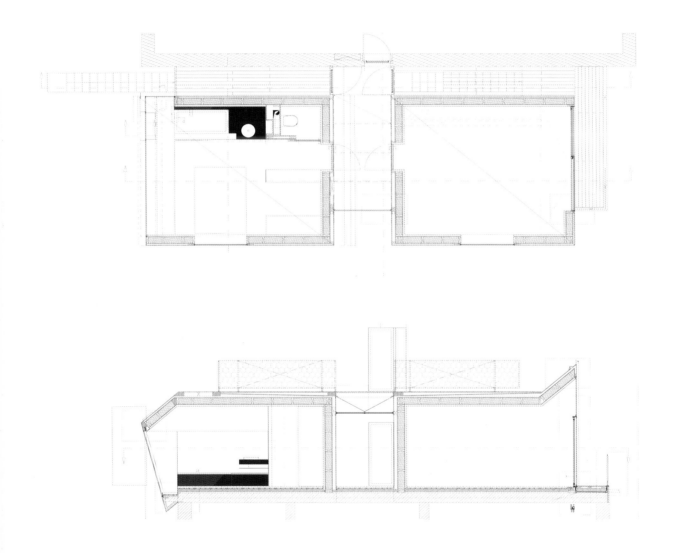

B HOUSE

Atelier A5

Tokyo, Japan

81 m² / 875 sq ft

© Sadahiro Shimizu/Atelier A5

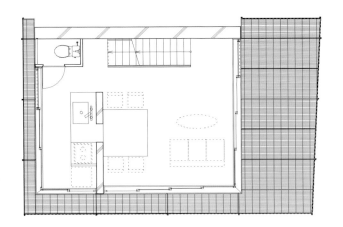

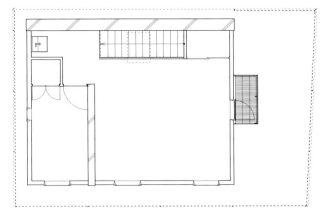

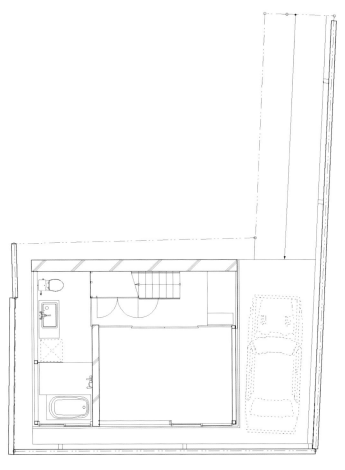

LAKE HOUSE

Bercy Chen Studio

Lago Vista, United States

© Joseph Pettyjohn

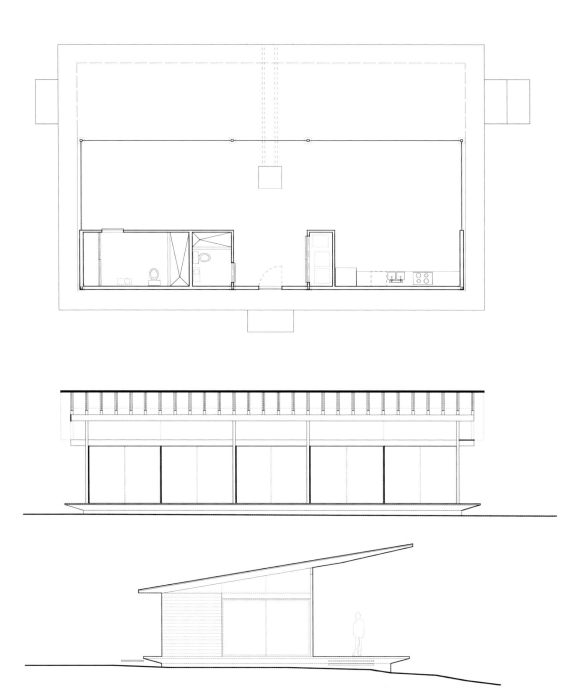

COPYPASTE HOUSE

UCX Architects

Alblasserdam, The Netherlands

© Rob't Hart

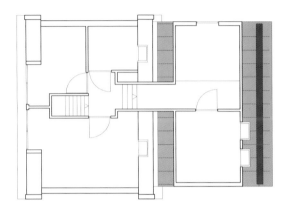

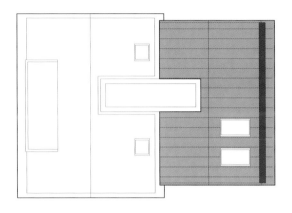

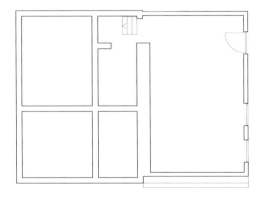

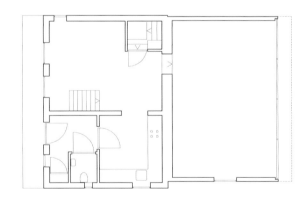

K BOX

Hirotaka Satoh

Tokyo, Japan

60 m² / 645 sq ft

© Hirotaka Satoh

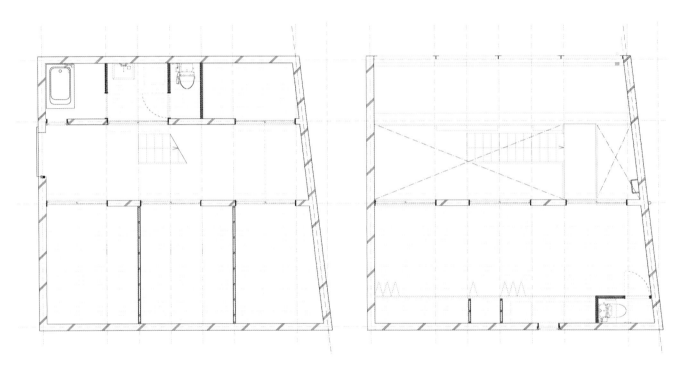

SWIFT

TreeHouse Company

Mid Wales, United Kingdom

© Chris Tubbs

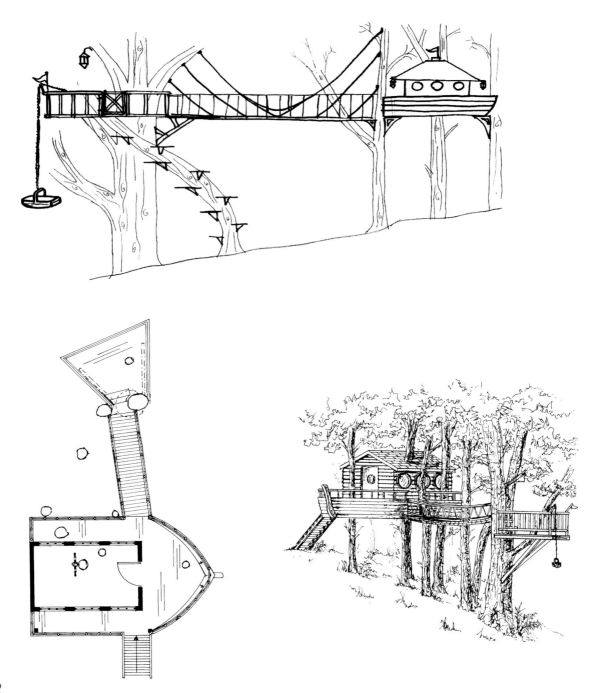

FREDERICKS

TreeHouse Company

West Sussex, United Kingdom

© TreeHouse Company

MATHEWS

TreeHouse Company

Oxford, United Kingdom

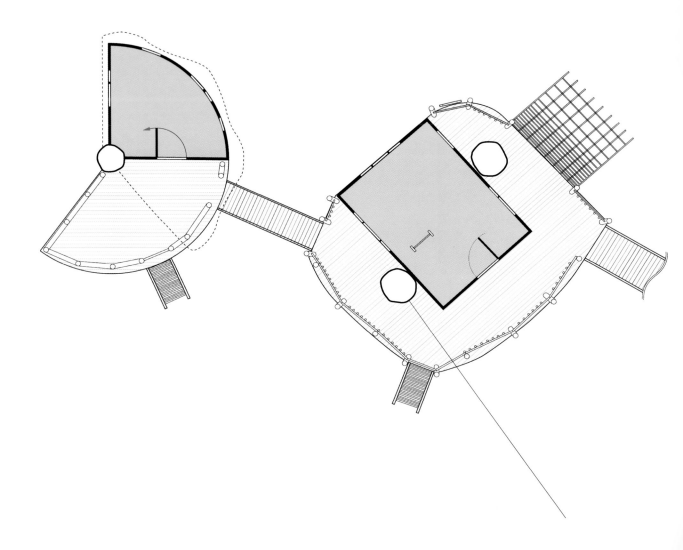

574

FALCON

TreeHouse Company

Fife, Scotland United Kingdom

© TreeHouse Company

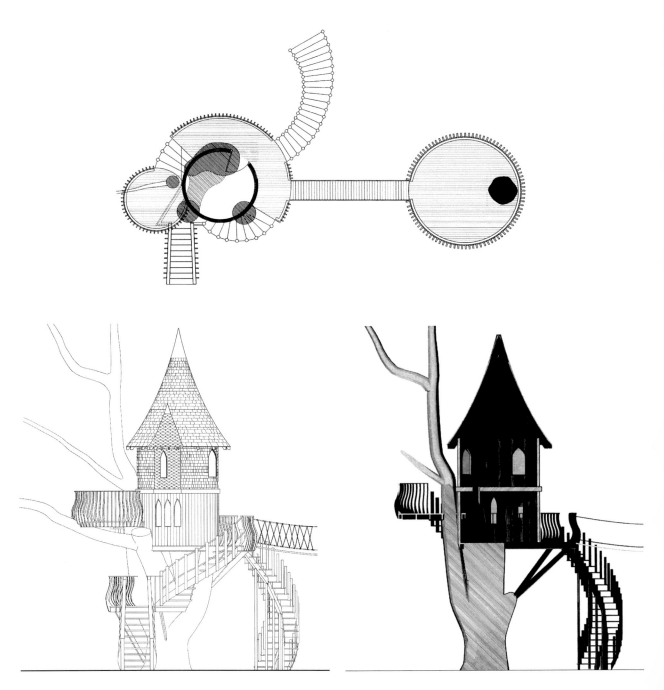

TRENDS
TENDENZEN
TENDANCES
TRENDS

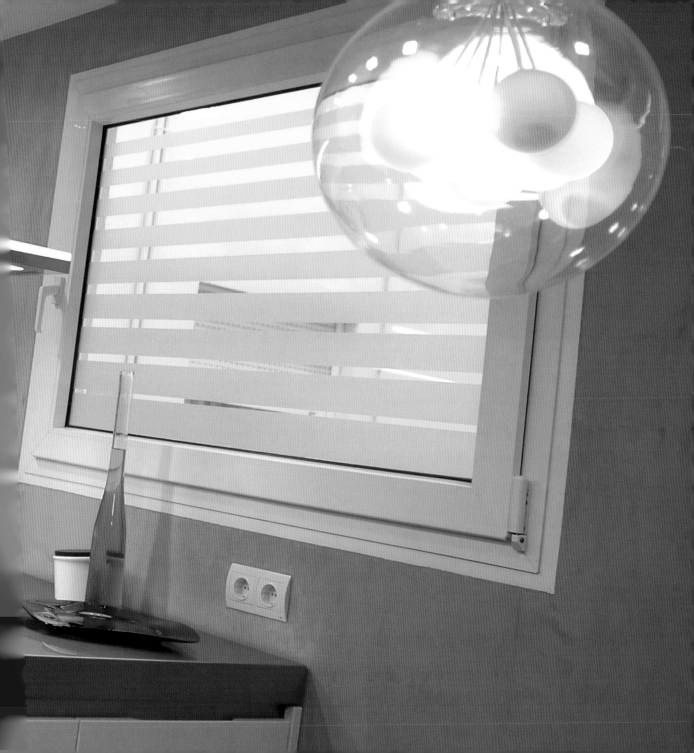

584-585
© Bonaldo

586 © Zanotta
587 © Viccarbe

588 © Klaessons
589 © Müller
Möbelfabrikation

590-591
© Klaessons

592 © Punt Mobles
593 © Tapeten der 70er

594-595
© La Oca

596-597
© Fritz Hansen

598-599
© Diego Fortunato

600-601
© Fritz Hansen

602-603
© Fritz Hansen

604-605
© Vitamin Living

606-607
© Bernat Martorell